THE ART
of
BREAKFAST

Down East

Published by Down East Books
An imprint of Globe Pequot
Trade division of The Rowman & Littlefield Publishing Group, Inc.
4501 Forbes Blvd., Ste. 200
Lanham, MD 20706
www.rowman.com
www.downeastbooks.com
Distributed by NATIONAL BOOK NETWORK

Names: Moos, Dana, author.
Title: The art of breakfast : B&B style recipes to make at home / Dana Moos.
Description: Camden, Maine : Down East Books, [2019] | Includes index.
Identifiers: LCCN 2019013643| ISBN 9781608935963 (cloth : alk. paper) | ISBN 9781608935970 (electronic)
Subjects: LCSH: Breakfasts. | Entertaining.
Classification: LCC TX733 .M664 2019 | DDC 641.5/2--dc23 LC record available at https://lccn.loc.gov/2019013643

∞™ The paper used in this publication meets the minimum requirements of American National Standard for Information Sciences—Permanence of Paper for Printed Library Materials, ANSI/NISO Z39.48-1992.

the art of breakfast

B&B-Style Recipes to Make at Home

DANA MOOS

BLUEBERRY OATMEAL
STREUSEL FRENCH
TOAST, *page 128*

T o my husband, Greg, who believed in me enough to leave the security of the job he held for more than twenty years and head to Maine to buy a bed and breakfast. Thank you so much for just letting me do my thing! And for being so patient when it comes to taking pictures of the food before we eat: "Will we be eating this while it's hot?" And for always being a step behind me to do my dishes. But mostly for being by my side. It's the little things that matter the most, and I appreciate them all.

To my friends and family who have always been supportive and encouraging and know I'm happy to cook for them any time. Thanks to Mom and Dad for introducing me to fine foods at a young age; I may not have fully appreciated it then, but I do now!

And many thanks to our former inn guests who always encouraged me to write a cookbook, who asked for recipes and took photos of our breakfasts. You've been an inspiration over the years.

Thank you all!

With much love, Dana

MUSHROOM SAUSAGE
STRATA, *page XX*

CONTENTS

INTRODUCTION

Like many, I find great joy and gratification in cooking and providing for guests—so much so that in 2004 my husband and I moved from the Washington, DC, suburbs, to Mount Desert Island to buy the Kingsleigh Inn in Southwest Harbor. Once there, I found helping to enhance my guests' vacations extremely satisfying, especially when it came to the food. Because we were too busy to serve dinner at the inn, I pushed the envelope when it came to gourmet three-course breakfasts. My feeling was that breakfast could be as special as fine dining in the evening.

Over my seven years as an innkeeper, I learned techniques to make things simple and easy to prepare in advance but without ever compromising quality. But more importantly, I learned how to make breakfast artful. Now when I walk through a food market, I see shelves filled with food to paint my canvas or empty plate. Fresh fruits and vegetables are my preferred medium. Butter, cream, and sugar are a close second. My favorite kitchen tool is a torch (and not a mini-torch; I'm talking a high-heat torch for soldering jobs!).

This book is about putting together common pantry ingredients in unique ways. It's about creating beautiful art on a plate by combining fresh fruits and vegetables in imaginative yet simple ways. It's about seeing food in colors, the way we learned from the color chart in elementary school. It's about looking at a plate of food as a composition and balancing colors, textures, and flavors. We don't just eat with our mouths; we eat with our eyes first. When you begin to appreciate food in this manner, you'll be able to grasp the basic principles of the art component of creating a fine dining experience during any meal.

When you create for friends and family, you share a bit of yourself. This is what I learned and most appreciated as an innkeeper: the art of providing and concierge. Something else I learned as an innkeeper is that you can't please all of the people all of the time. But I sure tried. I catered to vegetarians, low-carb diets, gluten-free diets, egg allergies, lactose intolerance—you name it. I wanted everyone to like everything I made! So when I created my menus, some days might have been heavy on the butter and sugar, while others were big on vegetables and low on carbs. Carnivores didn't even realize I rarely served meat because what they were enjoying was so much more creative and fresh. What I ended up with was something that I've been saying for years: everything in moderation. That's exactly what you'll find in this cookbook: freshness, indulgence, and moderation, never compromising taste, quality, or creativity.

So dig in. You'll find this book to be part epicurean education, part recipe collection, and part food photography—but most of all, a tool to inspire and spark your own culinary creativity.

Hopefully, you, your friends, and your family will enjoy what you'll learn on your journey with *The Art of Breakfast*. Bon appetit!

—*Dana Moos*

MINI BANANA BUNDT,
page 166

CHAPTER 1

Fruit Course

To me, a fruit course is all about flavor, texture, and color combinations. Its goal should be to awaken the taste buds. Some of my favorites are simply chilled fresh fruit dishes with herbed simple syrups. But sometimes warm, gooey caramelized pears are perfect on a chilly winter day. These fruit dishes also offer a nice lighter alternative for dessert. My favorite kitchen tool when it comes to the fruit course? A torch. So head straight to your local hardware store!

Caramelized Pineapple and Banana
with Cinnamon Crème

I clearly recall the very first dish I created for the inn's menu before we even moved to Maine. I put sliced bananas and pineapple in a flameproof dish, sprinkled it with cinnamon, topped it with brown sugar, and broiled for a couple minutes. When I realized that I had no control over the browning, my husband pulled out his torch. My pineapple and banana towers were born. But guests Noreen and Michael one morning claimed that they looked like cairns, the directional rock stacks that serve as hiking trail markers in nearby Acadia National Park. From that morning on, we put them on the inn's regular menu rotation and called them Pineapple Banana Cairns.

Serves 4

½ of a pineapple, peeled and cut into vertical quarters

2 ripe bananas

4 tablespoons Cinnamon Crème *(see page 188)*

4 tablespoons raw sugar

1. Cut the core off of each of the pineapple quarters. Slice 2 of the pineapple quarters and both bananas into about 10 ¼-inch slices. Layer, starting with the largest slices of pineapple on the bottom, stacking four pieces of each.

2. Top the tower with a tablespoon of cinnamon crème, then a tablespoon of sugar.

3. Carefully torch at a distance that will allow the sugar to burn evenly. This takes about 4 to 5 seconds (depending on the size of your flame) if the flame is about 2 to 3 inches from the sugar. You're looking for the sugar crystals to melt and then lightly burn. If they dissolve into the sauce before you can burn them, just layer another teaspoon of sugar and quickly torch again. You may have to adjust how close you hold the flame to the sugar. Keep the flame moving all over the sugar to avoid a hot spot. If the sugar starts to smoke, you may have just gone a microsecond too long and will end up with burned sugar. But you can just remove the sugar and start over! Just practice—it will take some getting used to, but it's worth it.

Dana's Tip
You're trying to melt the sugar with the flame before it starts to naturally dissolve in the wet sauce. You also want to ensure all sugar crystals are melted and meld together, which then allows the top surface of the sugar to burn and brown. When melted and then burned, the sugar crystals will essentially become a solid piece of hard candy instead of individual crystals. White sugar will not work, as the crystals are too small and will immediately dissolve in the sauce before you can even turn the torch on.

2

Grapefruit Brûlée *with* Vanilla Bean Crème

This dish was a Condé Nast travel writer favorite. I've enjoyed broiled grapefruit at many bed and breakfasts, but the sugar tends to melt before it broils, not allowing you to achieve a nice thick sugar crust. Using a torch gives you control of the burning. For those on cholesterol medication who can't eat grapefruit, orange slices bruléed with Vanilla Bean Crème taste just like an orange Creamsicle.

Serves 4

2 ruby red grapefruits

8 tablespoons Vanilla Bean Crème *(see page 189)*

8 tablespoons raw sugar

1. Halve each grapefruit and section with a grapefruit knife or tool. (I have a fabulous two-sided knife with a double blade that cuts along each side of the membrane. The other, curved end cuts the fruit from the rind.) Place 2 tablespoons of vanilla bean crème on top of each grapefruit half.

2. Sprinkle 2 tablespoons sugar over the sauce on each half and torch immediately. Work quickly to avoid the sugar dissolving before you are able to torch and burn. You may need to layer more sugar and torch again in order to get the right burn.

4

Dana's Tip

Don't do as I do: I learned that my glass dishes were not flameproof on the last morning of our third season at the inn. I had sixteen bowls with grapefruit halves, ready for the torching. I usually topped two at a time with sugar and then torched. I got to the second-to-last dish and I must have held the flame too close to the glass—it cracked and went all over the kitchen island, and shattered glass was tossed around into the bowls of ready-to-be-served fruit. Needless to say, I didn't serve a fruit course that morning; we went right into the entrée. That next season I bought new, flameproof dishes!

Watermelon and Kiwi *with* Coconut Lime Crème

This is one of the classic examples of fruits of opposite colors working beautifully together. The inspiration came from the use of lime and coconut in Thai foods. The lime adds such a delightful brightness to the dish and won't curdle the sour cream. I wanted to use a fruit of the opposite color to the watermelon and experimented with kiwi. I just had a feeling it was going to work. The kiwi is very acidic and the watermelon not so much; the sauce marries the two beautifully.

Serves 6

½ of a medium seedless watermelon (or a whole baby seedless melon)

8 kiwi

juice of 1 lime

½ cup Coconut Lime Crème
(see page 188)

zest of 1 lime, for garnish

1. Cut the rind from the watermelon and kiwi. Cut the watermelon into triangles about ¼ inch thick and about the size of an oversized tortilla chip. Cut the kiwi into slices ¼ inch thick. Refrigerate both until well chilled, about 45 minutes.

2. When ready to serve, stack on a dry plate, starting with the watermelon and alternating fruits. Squeeze about a teaspoon of lime juice onto each stack of fruit, then spoon a few tablespoons of the coconut lime crème over the top of the stack and onto the plate.

3. Garnish with a sprinkling of lime zest (pass the lime over the zester twice).

Grilled Peaches *with* Raspberry Coulis

This is my version of peach Melba—the cool raspberry coulis against the warm grilled peach is delicious! On warm days I prefer to serve the peaches chilled, with a scoop of frozen vanilla yogurt or raspberry sorbet.

Serves 4

4 medium-ripe large peaches

4 tablespoons toasted walnut oil (I love Fiore oils, but you can use any brand)

2 tablespoons granulated sugar

2 teaspoons white peach balsamic vinegar (again, Fiore has a fantastic one, or just use a white balsamic)

Raspberry Coulis *(see page 186),* **for garnish**

1. Halve and pit the peaches.
2. Drizzle the oil over the peach halves and dust with the sugar.
3. Grill the peaches over medium heat, flat side down, until you see some grill marks and char, about 10 minutes. Remove from the grill and place in container to rest for a couple of minutes. Evenly drizzle the vinegar while the peaches are still warm.
4. Drizzle the plate with raspberry coulis.

Roasted Plums *with* Thyme, Honey, and Vanilla Frozen Yogurt

The natural purple color when roasting the plums with the honey gives you an absolutely gorgeous and delicious translucent sauce to drizzle on a white plate. It's both sweet and tart. They make a great accompaniment to Ginger Spice Pancakes in the fall or winter. Roasting definitely enhances the color of this stone fruit. The sprinkle of fresh thyme just before serving looks lovely against the bright purple sauce.

Serves 4

2 tablespoons granulated sugar

3 tablespoons honey

4 firm black plums

1 sprig fresh thyme

vanilla frozen yogurt

> ### *Dana's Tip*
> *Warm the honey for about 25 seconds in a glass cup in the microwave so it spreads once you pour it onto the parchment. If the plums are softer to begin with, watch the cooking time because they'll cook faster. Once you see the exterior skin barely begin to wrinkle, it's time to remove them. You're better off removing them too soon as they will continue to soften slightly as they cool.*

1. Preheat the oven to 350 degrees.

2. Line a rimmed baking sheet with parchment paper a bit larger than the pan, to contain the juices.

3. Sprinkle the sugar on the parchment, then pour the honey onto the parchment.

4. Halve the plums and place cut side down on the sugar and honey.

5. Sprinkle half of the thyme leaves onto the honey; reserve the rest to garnish before serving.

6. Roast the plums for about 15 minutes, removing them from the oven just before they start to lose their shape or you see the skin wrinkle.

7. Place two halves in a bowl. Spoon some of the roasting liquid over the fruit. Add a scoop of vanilla frozen yogurt and sprinkle with the rest of the thyme leaves.

Cantaloupe *with* Green Tea–Infused Minted Simple Syrup

This is a surprisingly fresh combination of fruit and herbs where you still taste the true flavor of the melon. The fruit will soften after sitting in the syrup for a couple of days, so it is best eaten within twenty-four hours.

Serves 2 to 4

1 fresh cantaloupe, cut into small chunks
¼ cup Green Tea Mint–Infused Simple Syrup *(see page 184)*
fresh mint, for garnish

1. Toss the cantaloupe with the syrup and refrigerate for a couple of hours or until nicely chilled. Garnish with a fresh mint leaf.

CHILLED MOSCATA
POACHED PEARS,
page 10

Chilled Moscato Poached Pears

With honey and black pepper gorgonzola, hibiscus syrup, and toasted almonds

The sweet pears with the salty honey Gorgonzola make a really nice pair, and the black pepper offers a subtle unexpected note! And if you make extra pears, puree the poached pears with some of the poaching liquid and freeze for a really nice, quick pear sorbet.

Serves 4

4 ounces Gorgonzola cheese, room temperature

2 tablespoons honey

1½ teaspoons coarse cracked black pepper

¼ cup sliced almonds

4 firm Bosc pears

2 cups white cranberry juice

2 cups ginger ale

4 cups Moscato wine

1 cup granulated sugar

Hibiscus Syrup *(see page 183)*

1. Mix the Gorgonzola, honey, and pepper and set aside.

2. Toast almonds on a sheet pan at 300 degrees until fragrant and lightly browned, about 12–15 minutes.

3. Peel and core the pears.

4. In a deep saucepan, add the cranberry juice, ginger ale, wine, and sugar and bring to a boil. Add the pears; cover and lower heat to medium. Cook until tender, about 15 minutes. If the pears are riper to start, they'll require less cooking time. Use a paring knife inserted at the bottom to test for doneness.

5. Remove the pears and place in a container submerged in the poaching liquid and refrigerate. Serve chilled with the sweetened Gorgonzola, a drizzle of hibiscus syrup, and toasted almonds.

Port Wine Poached Pears

With chocolate ganache, balsamic vinegar, vanilla bean crème, and toasted pecans

Serves 4

¼ cup pecan halves
4 firm Bosc pears
4 cups cranberry juice
4 cups Ruby Port wine
1 cup granulated sugar
2 long cinnamon sticks, broken
6 star anise pods
1 teaspoon whole cloves
aged balsamic vinegar
Vanilla Bean Crème *(see page 189)*
Chocolate Ganache *(see page 186)*

1. Toast the pecans on a sheet pan at 300 degrees until fragrant, about 10–12 minutes.

2. Peel and core the pears.

3. In a deep saucepan, add the cranberry juice, wine, sugar, and spices and bring to boil. Add the pears; cover and lower heat to medium. Cook until tender, about 15 minutes. If the pears are riper to start, they'll require less cooking time. Use a paring knife inserted at the bottom to test for doneness.

4. Remove the pears and place in a container submerged in the poaching liquid and refrigerate. Serve chilled with a drizzle of balsamic, vanilla bean crème, and chocolate ganache.

Dana's Tip

If you're serving the pears chilled, they will soften slightly in the poaching liquid overnight, so you may want to undercook them by a couple of minutes or judge your cooking time based on the pears you find. This might take practice—if they end up too soft, use them for a batch of Pear Sorbet. Also, using star anise pods and cinnamon sticks as opposed to ground spices will keep your poaching liquid translucent and not cloudy like the ground spices would cause.

Madeira Wine Caramelized Pears

With candied almonds, pecans, pumpkin seeds, golden raisins, and cranberries, and honey blue cheese.

Serves 4

4 ounces Gorgonzola cheese

2 tablespoons honey

¼ teaspoon salt

½ teaspoon black pepper

2 firm Bosc or Bartlett pears

3 tablespoons butter

3 tablespoons Madeira

2 tablespoons raw sugar

2 tablespoons sliced almonds

1 tablespoon pumpkin seeds

2 tablespoons cranberries

1 tablespoon golden raisins

¼ teaspoon salt

1. Mix Gorgonzola, honey, salt, and pepper until smooth.

2. Cut each pear in half, and then cut each half into three sections.

3. Melt butter in large sauté pan over medium heat. Add pear quarters and sauté until lightly caramelized, about 4 minutes on each side. Remove pears and place 3 quarters on each plate and let sit while finishing the sauce.

4. Add the Madeira, raw sugar, nuts and seeds, cranberries, raisins, and salt and cook for about 3 minutes until the Madeira caramelizes with the fruit and nut and seed mixture, thickening slightly. Pour warm sauce/fruit and nut and seed mixture over pears. Serve with a small scoop of sweetened Gorgonzola.

Brûléed Fresh Figs with Vanilla Bean Crème *and* Balsamic Pearls

Pearls imported from Italy (Del Duca Perle from Fiore) make a wonderful addition to a cheese board. If you don't buy the pearls, then a drizzle of aged Balsamic is nice. Fiore started in Bar Harbor, Maine but various retailers carry similar products. Fiore does ship! See www.fioreoliveoils.com.

Serves 2 to 4

1 pint of fresh Black Mission or Brown Turkey figs (about 6–8)

6 tablespoons Vanilla Bean Crème *(see page 189)*

6 tablespoons raw sugar

1. Cut figs in half from stem to end.

2. Dip one half into the vanilla bean crème, then top with a tablespoon of raw sugar.

3. Torch until sugar is burned and very dark brown. Let cool before eating to avoid a burned mouth!

SALAD LYONNAISE,
page **24**

CHAPTER 2

Savory Small Plates, Bites, or Appetizers

In addition to a classic cheese and charcuterie board with crusty bread (one of my most favorite things in the world and good enough to be my last meal), try some of these bites that can go from a brunch buffet to the five o'clock happy hour or tailgate. It's tough to eat just one of my award-winning lobster wontons (as the judges claimed), and the bacon and onion jam will be a huge hit with your friends, family, and guests.

Lemon Zest Shrimp Salad

*With lemon zest, pickled red onion, and fresh dill
on brown bread*

Serves 6

2 pounds shrimp in the shell (deveined), small to medium size

1 tablespoon plus 1 teaspoon kosher salt

¾ cup mayonnaise

1 teaspoon Dijon mustard

1 teaspoon white wine vinegar

juice from ½ of a lemon

½ teaspoon freshly ground black pepper

2 tablespoons minced fresh dill

½ minced red onion

3 stalks minced celery

zest from the whole lemon

microgreens, for garnish

1 loaf of dark brown grain bread

1. Bring 4 quarts of water and 1 tablespoon salt to a boil in a large saucepan. Add the shrimp and reduce the heat to medium. Cook uncovered for 3 minutes or until the shrimp are just cooked through. Remove with a slotted spoon to a bowl of cold water. Let cool; then peel the shrimp.

2. In a separate bowl, whisk together the mayonnaise, mustard, vinegar, lemon juice, 1 teaspoon salt, pepper, and dill. Combine with the peeled shrimp. Add the red onion and celery and check the seasonings. Cover and refrigerate for a few hours so the flavors meld.

Pickled Onions

1 large red onion, halved through core, thinly sliced crosswise

½ cup sugar

½ cup white wine vinegar

1½ teaspoons coarse kosher salt

1½ teaspoons whole black peppercorns

To make the pickled onions:

Place the onion slices in a medium bowl. Bring remaining ingredients to a boil in a heavy medium-size saucepan. Pour over onions in the bowl. Cover and cool to room temperature. Chill overnight.

To assemble the dish:

1. Slice bread into ¼-inch slices and toast in oven until lightly crisped.

2. Top with a spoon of shrimp salad and a few slices of the pickled onion followed by a sprinkling of fresh dill, lemon zest, and microgreens.

Maine Lobster Salad on Puff Pastry

With fresh lemon, shallots, dill, and lemon zest mayo

The lemon really lightens this up.

Serves 4

2 cooked Maine lobsters, about 1¼ pounds each,
    cut into ½-inch chunks

½ cup mayonnaise

juice from 1 lemon, plus the zest from the lemon

1 large shallot, finely diced

1½ tablespoons fresh dill, minced

½ teaspoon sweet paprika

¾ teaspoon kosher salt

¼ teaspoon coarse black pepper

1 sheet of frozen puff pastry, thawed

1. Mix lobster, mayonnaise, lemon juice, the zest from half of the lemon, shallot, 1 tablespoon dill, paprika, salt, and pepper and refrigerate. Keep refrigerated to meld at least 2 hours.

2. Preheat the oven to 400 degrees.

3. Cut four 5-inch squares from the puff pastry sheet and reserve remaining dough for another use (or double the recipe for the lobster salad!). Place squares of puff pastry on a sheet pan lined with parchment or a silicone baking sheet. With a knife, score the dough around the edge and use a fork to prick holes in the center. This will keep the center from puffing up too much.

4. Bake until lightly browned, 12–15 minutes. Let cool 15 minutes. Top each puff pastry with lobster salad, zest from the remaining half lemon, and a sprinkling of dill from the remaining ½ tablespoon.

Smoked Salmon *and* Chive Goat Cheese Crostini

With red onions, lemon zest, and capers

Serves 12

1 fresh baguette, sliced on a bias, about ¼ inch thick

4 ounces goat cheese, softened

2 ounces cream cheese, softened

½ teaspoon salt

¼ teaspoon black pepper

2 tablespoons fresh minced chives

6 slices of thinly sliced smoked salmon

1 tablespoon red onion, finely diced

zest from 1 lemon

20

1. Toast baguette slices at 350 degrees for about 10–12 minutes until lightly toasted.

2. Mix goat cheese, cream cheese, salt, pepper, and 1½ tablespoons of the chives until well blended. This is best if mixed several hours before ready to use. Spread about a tablespoon of the goat cheese mixture onto each crostini.

3. Cut each slice of salmon in half and layer on top of the goat cheese mixture, then top with red onion and remaining chives. Using a fine zester, zest the lemon over top the crostini. For a more refined presentation, roll each piece of salmon and stand on end on top of crostini, as pictured.

Smoked Salmon, Caviar, Horseradish Crème Fraiche, *and* Fresh Dill on Cucumber or Zucchini Rounds

This is a beautiful garnish—almost too pretty to eat! It also makes an elegant hors d'oeuvre to enjoy with some bubbly.

Serves 10

1 medium or large cucumber or zucchini

½ cup crème fraiche

1 tablespoon bottled horseradish

2 sprigs fresh dill

¼ teaspoon salt

4 ounces smoked salmon

1 ounce caviar

1. Cut the cucumber or zucchini into ¾-inch rounds. Using a small melon baller, scoop out the very center, creating shallow cavities for the crème fraiche to sit in.

2. Mix together the crème fraiche, horseradish, ½ a sprig of chopped dill, and salt.

3. Place about ½ teaspoon of the crème fraiche onto a vegetable round, then roll up a 2-inch piece of salmon and place it on top, and add a ½ teaspoon caviar and a fresh sprig of dill to garnish.

Smoked Salmon, Cream Cheese, *and* Cucumber Roulade

I really love Ducktrap smoked salmon from Maine, but any thinly sliced cold smoked salmon will work. This makes a wonderful small accompaniment to an entrée. It's much more than just a beautiful garnish. Not a fan of cucumber? You can omit the cucumber in this roulade.

Serves 4

1 medium cucumber

8 2-inch by 4-inch thin slices of smoked salmon,

4 tablespoons cream cheese, softened at room temperature

4 pieces red- or green-leaf lettuce

1 lemon, thinly sliced, for garnish

1 fresh dill sprig, chopped (about 1 tablespoon)

juice of 1 lemon, for drizzling over top of salmon

1. Peel the cucumber and cut to 6 inches in length. Using the peeler, shave 8 thin strips of cucumber from end to end and place on a paper towel to absorb the moisture.

2. Place a slice of salmon on top of each cucumber slice.

3. Spread 1 tablespoon of the cream cheese on top of each slice of salmon.

4. Roll up and stand vertically, on edge, revealing the cut edge.

5. When ready to plate, place a small piece of lettuce and top with two salmon roulades, side by side, separated by a thin lemon slice. Add a sprinkle of dill and freshly squeezed lemon over the salmon.

Deviled Egg Duo

Smoked salmon, red onion, and caviar; smoked paprika and crispy bacon.

Makes 12 halves (6 of each)

6 large eggs
2 slices of thick-cut bacon
⅓ cup mayonnaise
1 teaspoon Dijon mustard
1 teaspoon yellow mustard
½ teaspoon white vinegar
dash of kosher salt
sweet paprika
smoked paprika
1 tablespoon capers
1 tablespoon diced red onion
1 slice smoked salmon, cut into
**   6 portions**
red or black caviar
zest from ½ a lemon
finely diced chives

1. Place the eggs in a pan of cold salted water. Bring to a boil and then cover and turn off the heat. Let sit, covered, 12 minutes. Drain and fill with cold water to help cool. Peel the eggs carefully under running water.

2. While the eggs are cooking, crisp the bacon, drain, and let cool, and dice finely.

3. Halve the eggs, scoop out the yolk, and place in small bowl. Mix in mayo, mustards, vinegar, and salt until very smooth (a food processor works best if you really want a smooth mixture). Place in a piping bag or clear baggie with a snipped end.

4. Season the egg white halves with a dash of salt first. Then dust 6 with the sweet paprika, 6 with the smoked paprika (this way, you see the egg instead of the paprika). Fill each egg with the egg mixture.

5. Top the 6 sweet paprika eggs with a few capers, a sprinkling of red onion, a small piece of smoked salmon, and a dollop of caviar. Finish the eggs with a few passes over a zester with a lemon half.

6. Top the 6 smoked paprika eggs with the cooked bacon and some fresh chives.

Salad Lyonnaise

This is a salad of mixed greens with bacon, fingerling potatoes, hard-boiled eggs, garlic ciabatta croutons, and a Dijon vinaigrette.

Serves 6

8 small new potatoes, cubed

6 large eggs

12 slices thick-cut bacon, cut into 1-inch pieces

8 cups torn frisèe, packed (you can use mixed greens if you can't find frisèe but try to include something peppery such as arugula)

2 tablespoons fresh parsley

2 teaspoons fresh chives

Garlic Croutons *(see recipe below)*

½ teaspoon freshly ground black pepper

1. Cook the potatoes in boiling salted water until just tender. Set aside to cool to room temperature.

2. Add eggs to a pot of cold salted water. Bring to a boil. Turn off heat, cover, and let sit 12 minutes. Add eggs to ice water and let sit for a few minutes until they cool. Peel and quarter the eggs.

3. Cook the bacon until only slightly crisp. Drain and set aside.

4. Toss the greens with the parsley and chives. Add the potatoes and bacon; add dressing just before serving and toss gently to avoid breaking up the eggs too much. Top with garlic croutons. Top with some freshly ground pepper.

Dijon Vinaigrette

1 cup good-quality mild olive oil

⅛ cup red wine vinegar

1 tablespoon fresh-squeezed lemon juice

2 tablespoons Dijon mustard

1 shallot, minced

1 garlic clove, minced on a zester

¼ teaspoon salt

1 tablespoon honey

freshly ground cracked pepper, to taste

To make the dressing:

1. Mix all ingredients until well blended, using either a hand whisk or blender.

Garlic Croutons

4 tablespoons butter

4 tablespoons olive oil

2 cloves of garlic, finely minced on a zester

dash of salt

1 loaf Italian ciabatta, cut into crouton-size pieces

To make the croutons:

1. Preheat the oven to 350 degrees.

2. Melt the butter and olive oil and heat just until incorporated. Add the garlic and salt. Toss the bread cubes in a bowl with the butter mixture and then spread them on a cookie sheet. Bake until crisp and lightly browned, about 20–25 minutes. Let cool.

Bacon, Onion, *and* Fig Jam

Makes about 1½ cups

3 medium onions, diced

½ stick butter

8 slices thick-cut slab bacon, diced

4 fresh figs (dried are fine as well) plus 4 dried figs, diced

3–4 tablespoons light brown sugar

2 tablespoons fig balsamic vinegar

1 tablespoon espresso balsamic vinegar

2 tablespoons whole-grain mustard (I used my favorite, Maille)—*not stone ground*

½ teaspoon kosher salt

½ teaspoon freshly cracked pepper

1–2 teaspoons of sugar, if needed, to taste.

1. Sauté the onions with butter in large saucepan over medium-low heat until they begin to brown, about 45 minutes.

2. While the onions are cooking, cook the bacon until it's just shy of crisp; you want some "bend" to remain (about 80 percent done). Add to the onions, adding some, but not all, of the grease. Then stir in the remaining ingredients and simmer on low for about 20 minutes. Taste after about 10 minutes. If it's not sweet enough, add sugar. If it's not tart enough, add more fig balsamic vinegar. If you want a savory kick, add more mustard. This is where you cook to your taste.

Here's one way to enjoy your new favorite jam: Top baguette slices (either fresh or baked until crisp) with blue cheese butter (*see recipe below*) and a spoonful of bacon jam. This is a really lovely balance between sweet and savory.

Blue Cheese Butter

8 ounces blue cheese (I used Gorgonzola)

½ stick butter

To make the blue cheese butter:

1. Let cheese and butter sit at room temperature to soften. Mix with paddle attachment in stand mixer or food processor (or by hand!) until well combined.

Savory Spinach and Parmesan Tart
(Gluten-Free/Vegetarian)

Imagine a frittata and quiche meet spinach Parmesan dip—it's quite addictive! It's great for an afternoon appetizer, light brunch, or lunch with a salad. On occasion at the inn I liked to serve a small slice of this alongside a sweet crepe, sliced crusty bread, or focaccia to satisfy the sweet and savory preference. For gluten-free version, eliminate the panko break crumbs.

Serves 12

Crust

¾ stick butter, melted

¾ cup panko bread crumbs

¼ cup shredded Parmesan cheese

Filling

2 shallots, finely diced

1 tablespoon olive oil

2 cloves garlic, finely minced

1 10-ounce bag fresh baby spinach

1 bunch scallions

4 eggs

3 8-ounce packages cream cheese, softened

¼ cup sour cream

4 ounces goat cheese

1 tablespoon Dijon mustard

½ teaspoon salt

½ teaspoon freshly ground black pepper

⅛ teaspoon cayenne pepper

1 teaspoon dry mustard

1 cup shredded Parmesan cheese

½ cup grated Parmesan cheese

½ cup shredded Swiss cheese

1. Preheat the oven to 350 degrees.

2. Mix the melted butter with breadcrumbs and Parmesan and press into bottom of 9-inch springform pan. Bake for 10 minutes.

3. Sauté the shallots in the olive oil over medium heat until soft and lightly browned, about 10 minutes. Add the garlic and cook, stirring, for 30 seconds. Remove from the pan and place in a large bowl.

4. Add the spinach to the same pan, cover, and cook over medium-low heat for 3 minutes. Remove and pat dry. Chop and add to the shallots.

5. Thinly slice the scallions and add them to the shallot and spinach mixture.

6. In a mixing bowl, beat the eggs on medium speed. Add the cream cheese, sour cream, goat cheese, mustard, salt, pepper, cayenne, and dry mustard and mix for 10–15 seconds until well combined.

7. Add the Parmesan and Swiss cheeses and the spinach mixture to the eggs and mix on low speed for 5 seconds.

8. Pour into the springform pan on top of the cooked bread crumbs and bake for about an hour, until the center is set. Allow to cool for about 10 minutes before slicing.

Tomato, Ricotta, *and* Swiss Tarts

Another wonderful appetizer, but we served it as a decadent accompaniment to eggs at the inn. It would also make a lovely lunch with a salad. Pastry, cheese, and tomatoes? I'm happy.

Makes 9 to 10 tarts

5 plum tomatoes, halved

2 tablespoons olive oil

¼ teaspoon salt

a few turns of freshly ground black pepper

1 package refrigerated pie dough

1 egg, beaten

1 cup ricotta cheese

2 cloves garlic, finely minced

¼ cup grated Parmesan cheese

¼ cup shredded Parmesan cheese

½ cup shredded Swiss cheese

1 small sprig of fresh thyme, leaves stripped

½ teaspoon salt

1. Preheat the oven to 375 degrees.

2. Place the tomato halves on a baking sheet, sprinkle on the olive oil, salt, and pepper, and roast for an hour.

3. Meanwhile, using a biscuit cutter about 3 inches round, cut the crust into 9 discs. Roll out the remaining dough to the same thickness and cut into 1–2 more discs. Coat a muffin tin with nonstick cooking spray and place a disc of dough at the base of each one. The disc should come up the sides just a bit. Brush the edges of the dough with the beaten egg wash and bake for 10 minutes.

4. Mix the ricotta, garlic, and grated Parmesan together until well blended. Add a tablespoon to each section of the muffin tin. Add about ½ tablespoon each of shredded Parmesan and Swiss cheeses. Top with the tomato halves and thyme leaves.

5. Lower the oven to 350 degrees and bake until bubbly and lightly browned, about 20 minutes.

Lobster Wontons

Fried wontons, smoked butter aioli with charred scallions and truffle oil, lobster, and a soy glaze—this is a double-award-winning recipe! First place in Judge's and People's Choice for Best Lobster Bite at the 2018 7th Annual Boothbay Harbor (Maine) Claw Down competition!

Makes 32

black and white sesame seeds

vegetable oil for frying

16 wonton wrappers, cut in half

1 lb fresh picked lobster meat, portioned into 32 half-ounce portions

minced chives, for garnish

1. Toast the sesame seeds on a parchment-lined sheet pan in a 300-degree oven until the white sesames have a light golden hue, about 10–12 minutes. Let cool.

2. Add an inch or so of vegetable oil to a deep fry or sauté pan. When the oil is 375 degrees, add 4–5 wontons at a time and cook for about a minute, until golden brown on each side. Set aside on a towel and season with kosher salt. Let cool and store in airtight container.

Smoked Truffle Aioli

Makes about 2 cups

1 bunch of scallions (about 6–8), bottoms trimmed

1 tablespoon olive oil, for grilling scallions

1½ cups Japanese "Kewpie" mayonnaise (This is made from egg yolks, not whole eggs like traditional American mayonnaise, so it's creamier. You can find it online or in Asian markets.)

½ stick butter

½ teaspoon salt plus ¼ teaspoon for tossing on scallions

1 teaspoon black pepper

1 tablespoon white truffle oil

To make the aioli:

1. Drizzle the scallions with the olive oil, sprinkle with salt, and grill over medium heat until really well charred, about 10 minutes. Roughly chop and set aside.

2. For the smoking you can use either an outdoor smoker or a stovetop smoker. I used a Cameron stovetop smoker, but I used it on the grill since I had to grill my scallions and the grill was already hot.

3. Place 1 cup of the mayonnaise and butter in an ovenproof dish and place in smoker (following manufacturer instructions). Smoke for about 30 minutes. If it has been adequately smoked, you'll see browned bits along the edge of the baking dish and a light brown tint to the mayo and butter. Let cool. Add to blender with the remaining mayonnaise, salt, black pepper, and truffle oil. Add the scallions and blend until scallions are in small bits but still very visible. Store in squeeze bottle.

Soy Glaze

Makes 1 cup

¼ cup dark brown sugar

¼ cup sweet soy sauce (which is thicker, similar to molasses, and can be found in Asian markets)

¼ cup regular soy sauce

2 tablespoons rice cooking wine

2 tablespoons medium sherry

1 teaspoon rice wine vinegar

1 tablespoon mirin

1½ teaspoons molasses

1½ teaspoons fish sauce

1 tablespoon honey

To make the soy glaze:

1. Add the brown sugar, soy sauces, rice wine, sherry, and rice vinegar to a small saucepan and heat until brown sugar is dissolved. Remove from heat. Stir in remaining ingredients. Let cool and store in squeeze bottle.

To assemble the dish:

Squeeze the aioli onto the wonton, from end to end. Top with ½ ounce of lobster chunks, a drizzle of soy glaze, a sprinkling of chives, and toasted sesames. Don't be shy on the sauces—they are key to the flavor explosion!

Charred Scallion Lobster Crepes

Smoked truffle aioli, sweet soy glaze, fried wonton bits, toasted sesames, chives, and microgreens—another award-winning recipe, this one from the 2018 Maine Lobster Chef of the Year competition at Harvest on the Harbor in Portland, Maine!

Makes about 14 crepes

Batter

½ stick butter plus more for greasing the crepe pan

2 bunches of scallions

olive oil for grilling scallions

5 large eggs

1¼ cups 2% milk

1 cup all-purpose flour

1 teaspoon salt

1 teaspoon sugar

½ teaspoon mustard powder

½ teaspoon onion powder

1 teaspoon dried chives

½ teaspoon black pepper

1 tablespoon Soy Glaze *(see page 33)*

Brown Butter Poached Lobster

1 pound lobster meat, raw and picked

1½ sticks of butter

Garnish

microgreens

chives, finely diced

toasted black and white sesames

fried wonton bits

Smoked Truffle Aioli *(see page 32)*

Soy Glaze *(see page 33)*

1. In small saucepan, add ½ stick butter and cook over medium-low heat until lightly brown in color and milk solids have fully separated, about 8–10 minutes, watching very carefully not to burn the butter. Strain through fine mesh sieve and set aside.

2. In a large sauté pan, add 1½ sticks butter and heat over medium-low for 1 minute. Add lobster and cook until lobster is fully opaque, but cook slowly to avoid overcooking, about 6–8 minutes. Set aside.

3. Heat grill and cook scallions with lid closed on medium-low, flipping halfway through, until charred, about 8–10 minutes. Set aside to cool. Chop into small pieces, about an inch or less.

4. In a blender, add eggs, milk, flour, salt, sugar, mustard powder, onion powder, chives, black pepper, and soy glaze. Blend on medium, scrape down the sides, and blend another few seconds. Then add the melted butter through the lid opening and blend another few seconds. On medium-low, add scallions and blend until scallions are in very small bits, about 5 seconds. Let the batter rest at least 4 hours or as long as overnight. Bring to room temperature before making crepes.

5. Heat a crepe pan or a very shallow 8–9-inch sauté pan on medium-low until hot. Add about ½ tablespoon butter. After butter has melted, pour ⅓ cup of batter into the center of the pan. Immediately pick up the pan and tilt and swirl it to spread the batter evenly over the bottom. Cook for 1½–2 minutes, or until the crepe is golden on the bottom. When you see the edge begin to brown, you know it's time to flip. Cook another 30 seconds on the other side. Set aside on wax paper. Cook remaining crepes, adding butter to pan as needed (at least every other crepe or more). I stack mine without wax paper between and have never found the need to place wax paper between crepes—and I've stacked nearly one hundred crepes in a stack!

6. Toast sesames on a parchment-lined sheet pan in a 300-degree oven until the white sesames have a light golden hue, about 10–12 minutes. Let cool.

7. Cut wontons into small ⅛–¼-inch squares and fry in vegetable oil at 360 degrees until golden. Drain on a paper towel and store in an airtight container.

To assemble the dish:

Quarter-fold the warm crepe. Top with the butter poached lobster. Drizzle both the aioli and soy glaze over top. Garnish with toasted sesames, microgreens, and a nice scattering of the wonton bits. If your crepes are cool, quarter-fold them and warm in a sauté pan with butter, 2 minutes per side, before topping.

Dana's Tip
When you are done with the lobster, keep the butter for a lobster stew base!

36

LOBSTER WONTONS,
page 32

**CHARRED SCALLION
LOBSTER CREPES,**
page 34

LOBSTER AND GRITS,
page 70

CHAPTER 3

Savory Mains

Egg Roulade *with* Sautéed Leeks, Parmesan, Lobster, *and* Sherry Butter

Roulade simply means "rolled." This is constructed just like a jelly roll cake on a sheet pan, but with egg; it's basically a rolled and baked omelet. The results are worth the extra steps. This version was our signature savory dish at the inn, a particular favorite for the chunks of fresh Maine lobster on top. (Thanks to my brother Glen for the idea to add this Maine crustacean to the dish. The sherry butter was all me!) This is one of the most indulgent entrées we served, but it was worth every calorie and every penny. We even received a recipe request from *Gourmet* magazine, but unfortunately our recipe didn't make it into the magazine before we had to say farewell to the publication. So here it is.

Serves 6

8 large eggs

2 cups plus 2 tablespoons heavy cream

1 teaspoon salt, divided

2 tablespoons extra-virgin olive oil

3 large leeks, washed and thinly sliced

1 8-ounce package cream cheese

1 teaspoon Worcestershire sauce

juice from ¼ lemon

1 stick plus 3 tablespoons butter

1½ cups shredded Parmesan cheese

½ cup dry sherry

16 ounces fresh, cooked lobster meat, cut into small chunks

1 10-ounce package baby spinach, washed and dried

fresh chopped chives, for garnish

> **Dana's Tip**
>
> *The size of the pan is imperative to the successful rolling of the egg—believe me, I tried several pan sizes and ratios of eggs to cream. This is it. No substitutes!*

1. Preheat the oven to 350 degrees.

2. Grease a rimmed heavy-duty half sheet pan (18x13) with butter or vegetable oil, line with parchment paper, and then grease the parchment, making sure to press it flat to the surface of the pan, leaving at least an inch overhang.

3. In a blender, mix the eggs, 2 cups of cream, and ½ teaspoon salt on high speed for 4–5 seconds. Pour the mixture into the lined baking sheet. Bake until you begin to see the surface of the egg just start to brown, about 25 minutes. Remove and let cool.

4. While cooling, heat the olive oil in a pan over medium-high heat. Sauté the leeks,

covered, until soft, about 10–12 minutes. When soft, add the cream cheese, Worcestershire sauce, the remaining 2 tablespoons of cream, lemon juice, and the remaining ½ teaspoon of salt and stir. When the cream cheese is thoroughly incorporated, add 3 tablespoons of butter, mix in, and remove from heat. Let cool for about 3 minutes.

5. Dollop small amounts of the leek filling onto the egg. Using an offset spatula, carefully spread the mixture over the entire egg sponge, trying not to tear the egg, as it is very delicate. Sprinkle the Parmesan over the filling, just like you're topping a pizza.

6. Here's the fun part: the rolling. With the short edge of the pan closest to you and using the parchment as a guide, roll the egg up onto itself (like a jelly roll cake) until you end up with the egg seam on the underside of the roll. Keep the egg covered with the parchment left after rolling as this will help keep the egg moist. Cover the entire roll with aluminum foil and bake for another 20 minutes.

7. While baking, melt the remaining stick of butter in a pan with the sherry and cook for about 5 minutes, allowing much of the alcohol to burn off. Then add the lobster, lower the heat, and cover. Simmer for 5 minutes.

8. To serve, place a pile of fresh baby spinach on a plate. Slice the roulade into 4–6 slices, layer onto the spinach, and top with a couple of spoonfuls of the lobster butter. Garnish with fresh chives.

Egg Roulade Filled *with* Ricotta, Fontina, Roasted Roma Tomatoes, *and* Garlic

This version is for ricotta lovers! It's creamy and balanced with fresh basil and caramelized roasted tomatoes. Buon Appetito!

Serves 6

8 large eggs

2 cups plus 2 tablespoons heavy cream

1 teaspoon salt, divided

4 Roma or Italian tomatoes

3 tablespoons extra-virgin olive oil

8 ounces of whole milk ricotta

2 cloves of garlic, finely minced

¼ cup grated Parmesan cheese

½ teaspoon salt

1 teaspoon black pepper

1½ cups shredded fontina

¼ cup basil leaves, torn

baby mixed greens

42

1. Preheat the oven to 350 degrees.

2. Grease a rimmed heavy-duty half sheet pan (18×13) with butter or vegetable oil, line with parchment paper, and then grease the parchment, making sure to press it flat to the surface of the pan, leaving at least an inch overhang.

3. In blender, mix the eggs, 2 cups of cream, and ½ teaspoon salt on high speed for 4–5 seconds. Pour the mixture into the lined baking sheet. Bake until you begin to see the surface of the egg just start to brown, about 25 minutes. Remove and set aside to cool.

4. Increase oven temperature to 400 degrees.

5. Chop the tomatoes into medium dice and toss with olive oil and salt. Place on a parchment-lined baking sheet and roast for 30 minutes. Let cool at least 10 minutes.

6. Mix ricotta, garlic, grated Parmesan, salt, and black pepper. Using an offset spatula, carefully spread the mixture over the entire egg sponge, trying not to tear the egg, as it is very delicate.

7. Sprinkle the shredded fontina, basil, and cooled roasted tomatoes.

8. With the short edge of the pan closest to you and using the parchment as a guide,

roll the egg up onto itself (like a jelly roll cake), until you end up with the egg seam on the underside of the roll. Keep the egg covered with the parchment left after rolling as this will help keep the egg moist. Cover the entire roll with aluminum foil, reduce oven back to 350 degrees, and bake for another 20 minutes.

9. Slice into 6 slices and serve atop the bed of baby salad greens. Garnish with fresh basil.

Egg Roulade *with* Bacon, Tomato, and Smoked Cheddar

This roulade is filled with sautéed bacon, onion, and tomato and topped with shredded smoked cheddar and regular sharp cheddar. Other variations might include layering pesto and herbed cheese with Parmesan, sun-dried tomatoes, or any vegetables. Just be sure to sauté your vegetables first so that the moisture doesn't come out in the roulade during the second baking.

Serves 6

8 large eggs

2 cups plus 2 tablespoons heavy cream

1 teaspoon salt, divided

4 Roma or Italian tomatoes

3 tablespoons extra-virgin olive oil

1 teaspoon dried, granulated garlic

6 strips thick-cut bacon

1 large yellow onion

4 ounces smoked cheddar, grated

8 ounces sharp cheddar, grated

baby mixed greens

18 cherry tomatoes, halved, for garnish

1. Preheat the oven to 350 degrees.

2. Grease a rimmed heavy-duty half sheet pan (18×13) with butter or vegetable oil, line with parchment paper, and then grease the parchment, making sure to press it flat to the surface of the pan, leaving at least an inch overhang.

3. In blender, mix the eggs, 2 cups of cream, and ½ teaspoon salt on high speed for 4–5 seconds. Pour the mixture into the lined baking sheet. Bake until you begin to see the surface of the egg just start to brown, about 25 minutes. Remove and set aside to cool.

4. Increase oven temperature to 400 degrees.

5. Chop the tomatoes into medium dice and toss with olive oil, salt, and garlic. Place on a parchment-lined baking sheet and roast for 30 minutes.

6. Meanwhile, chop the bacon and sauté until crisp and brown. Remove from bacon grease and set into small bowl. Chop the onion into small dice and add to the bacon

grease. Sauté over medium heat until lightly browned, about 15 minutes. Let the onions and tomatoes cool for about 10 minutes.

7. Sprinkle the cheese and freshly ground black pepper to taste. Evenly spread the tomatoes, onions, and ¾ of the bacon over top.

8. With the short edge of the pan closest to you and using the parchment as a guide, roll the egg up onto itself (like a jelly roll cake), until you end up with the egg seam on the underside of the roll. Keep the egg covered with the parchment left after rolling as this will help keep the egg moist. Cover the entire roll with aluminum foil, reduce oven back to 350 and bake for another 20 minutes.

9. Slice into 6 slices and serve atop the bed of baby salad greens. Garnish with the remaining bacon and cherry tomatoes.

Chive *and* Cream Cheese Scrambled Eggs in Baked Wonton

This is a fun and delightful way to serve simple scrambled eggs. Add salsa, cheddar, and some crumbled spicy sausage and you have a nice Latin American–inspired breakfast.

Serves 4

vegetable oil, for coating the popover pan

16 wonton wrappers

12 large eggs

1 cup heavy cream

2 tablespoons butter

1 bunch chives, finely diced

1 8-ounce package cream cheese

¼ teaspoon salt

freshly ground black pepper

thinly sliced scallions, for garnish

1. Preheat the oven to 350 degrees.

2. Liberally coat a popover pan with vegetable oil. Take 3–4 wonton wrappers for each popover cavity and line it, overlapping the wrappers. Be sure to get a wrapper into the bottom.

3. Bake until the tops are lightly browned, about 15 minutes. Then cover carefully with foil and bake another 15 minutes. This allows the wonton wrappers inside the pan to continue browning without overbrowning the edges. Let the wrappers sit to cool a few minutes and place each on individual serving plates.

4. Mix the eggs and the cream in blender for 5 seconds.

5. Add 2 tablespoons of butter to a large frying pan. Place pan over medium heat, and when butter is melted, pour the eggs and chives into pan and slowly cook until eggs are almost scrambled.

6. Add the cream cheese in small dollops and continue to cook until the eggs are set, just another minute or so, trying not to allow the cream cheese to completely melt into the eggs. Add salt and pepper to taste.

7. To serve, portion ¼ of the eggs in each wonton cup. You could serve this version with salsa on the side and a few slices of ripe avocado and fresh heirloom tomatoes.

Fluffy Frittata with Asparagus, Caramelized Shallots, *and* Goat Cheese

This recipe holds up well in a warm oven for an extended period of time, likely due to the heavy cream. I don't incorporate my toppings into the frittata, so that if an item is not to someone's taste, it can be removed without ruining the whole dish for them. I use fiddleheads when they're in season in Maine during a few weeks in early spring. Fiddleheads are the unfurled fronds of a fern, and several varieties are harvested; cinnamon ferns are one of them. I think they are similar in taste and texture to a combination of asparagus and broccolini.

Serves 8

18 large eggs

2 cups heavy cream

1 teaspoon dry mustard

½ teaspoon granulated onion powder

1 teaspoon salt

2 tablespoons extra-virgin olive oil

4 shallots, diced

1½ to 2 cups asparagus or fiddleheads, cut into 1-inch pieces

6 ounces goat cheese

freshly ground black pepper

1. Mix the eggs, cream, dry mustard, onion powder and salt in blender for about 4–5 seconds. (A blender really incorporates air and increases the volume dramatically.)

2. Preheat the oven to 325 degrees.

3. In a small skillet over low-medium heat, add the olive oil and sauté the shallots until caramelized, about 16–18 minutes.

4. Steam the asparagus in the microwave in a bowl covered with a wet paper towel for 1½ minutes or blanch in boiling water for 2 minutes. (If using fiddleheads, boil the fiddleheads until tender, about 15 minutes, and drain.)

5. Heat an ovenproof 12-inch nonstick skillet over medium-high heat. Add the egg mixture and stir constantly with a heatproof rubber spatula until curds form. Once you see curds form, quickly lower the heat and continue to move the eggs around, never stopping, almost as if to scramble. Remove from heat when the eggs are about half set. This helps the bottom from cooking in place and browning. A traditional frittata is intentionally browned; mine is not and remains fluffy and creamy.

6. Place on the center rack in the oven for about 10 minutes.

7. Remove from the oven and top with the goat cheese, shallots, asparagus, and a few grinds of freshly cracked black pepper. Finish in the oven for another 10 minutes, just until the toppings warm slightly but the egg does not overcook.

8. Let sit 5 minutes before slicing and serving (as you would a lasagna) so it will hold together, as the egg is very tender.

Dana's Tip

Try a variation of this recipe and top with
Parmesan, ricotta, cherry tomatoes, and fresh basil.

Sausage, Mushroom, and Gruyère Strata *with* Madeira Caramelized Onions

This is comfort food all the way. It's full of flavor and makes a lovely breakfast or lunch with a mixed greens salad and a light vinaigrette.

Serves 8

8 ounces sweet sausage, not in casings or casings removed

4 tablespoons butter, divided

4 tablespoons olive oil

8 ounces sliced cremini or white button mushrooms

2 medium onions, finely diced

½ cup medium-dry Madeira

1 teaspoon kosher salt, divided

1-pound loaf of challah or egg bread/brioche, cubed in 1-inch pieces

1 cup Gruyère

8 large eggs

1½ cups whole milk

1½ cups half and half

¼ teaspoon pepper

½ teaspoon ground mustard

½ teaspoon Hungarian sweet paprika

¼ cup grated Parmesan cheese

1. In a large sauté pan, cook crumbled sausage over medium heat until fully cooked through, about 10–12 minutes. Remove to small bowl. In the same pan, add 2 tablespoons each of butter and olive oil and sauté mushrooms until softened and lightly browned, about 10–12 minutes. Add to bowl with sausage.

2. In same frying pan, add the remaining butter and olive oil and sauté onions over medium heat until lightly browned, about 12–15 minutes. Add Madeira and cook to burn off the alcohol, about 5 minutes. Add to bowl with other sautéed ingredients. Add ½ teaspoon salt or to taste.

3. Butter a deep 9×13 or 3.5–4-quart baking dish and layer a third of the bread cubes. Then add a third of the sausage mixture to the top, and sprinkle with a third of the Gruyere. Repeat with two more layers.

4. In a blender, mix the eggs, milk, half and half, remaining ½ teaspoon salt, pepper,

mustard, paprika, and Parmesan until well blended, about 5 seconds. Pour over top the dish and refrigerate, covered, at least 8 hours or as long as overnight.

5. Preheat the oven to 350 degrees.

6. Let dish sit at room temperature for about 45 minutes before baking. Bake covered for 30 minutes, then uncover and continue to bake another 15 minutes, or until top is nicely browned. Then let rest for 5–10 minutes, covered, until ready to plate.

Lobster Bread Pudding *with* Sherry, Cognac, *and* Mascarpone

This is an absolutely delicious way to enjoy leftover lobster—if there is any!—for breakfast, brunch, or lunch.

Serves 4 (in individual 1-cup ramekins or baking dishes)

8 ounces cooked lobster meat (claw separated from tail and knuckle)

2 large shallots, finely diced

1 tablespoon olive oil

2 tablespoons butter, plus 2 tablespoons for buttering the ramekins

½ cup cognac

1 tablespoon tomato paste

4 ounces mascarpone, softened

1 tablespoon medium dry sherry

1 tablespoon chives, plus some for garnish

1½ teaspoons salt, divided

½ teaspoon pepper

3 large eggs

2 egg yolks

1½ cups heavy cream

½ cup half and half

1 teaspoon fresh thyme leaves

8 ounces of brioche bread or challah, cubed, preferably day-old and stale

1. Butter individual 1-cup baking dishes.

2. Coarsely chop the lobster tail and knuckle meat. Finely chop the claw meat and keep it separate.

3. Sauté the shallots in butter and olive oil over medium heat until lightly browned, about 10 minutes. Add the cognac and either ignite to burn off alcohol or cook for 5 minutes to allow most of it to cook off. Add the claw meat and tomato paste during the last 2 minutes of cooking. Let cool 5–10 minutes.

4. Mix mascarpone with sherry, chives, ½ teaspoon salt, and pepper.

5. In a blender, mix the eggs, yolks, cream, half and half, and 1 teaspoon salt until well blended. Fold in thyme leaves.

6. In a large bowl, mix the egg/cream mixture with the bread cubes. Add the shallot/cognac/lobster mixture and toss.

7. Place some of the bread custard mixture in each baking dish, filling about halfway. Dollop some mascarpone mixture and some lobster chunks, then top with more bread custard mixture and a few more lobster chunks.

8. Bake covered at 325 degrees for 35 minutes, then uncover and bake for another 10 minutes. Top with more diced chives.

Basic Savory Crepes

These are a few of my favorite things . . . for breakfast, brunch, lunch, or a light dinner paired with a salad and glass of white wine or bubbly.

Makes 12 crepes

1⅓ cups milk (I use 2%)
4 large eggs
1⅓ cups flour
pinch of salt
½ stick butter, melted

1. Mix the milk, eggs, flour, and salt in a blender, scraping down the sides to incorporate all the ingredients. Pour the melted butter through the opening in the lid and mix for another few seconds. Let the batter sit in the refrigerator at least 30 minutes or up to one day.

2. Remove the batter from refrigerator and let sit at room temperature for 30–60 minutes. Heat a shallow nonstick frying pan or steel crepe pan, 8–9 inches in diameter, over medium-high heat. Coat with nonstick cooking spray or butter. Add a small amount of batter and swirl it around to coat the pan in a thin layer. Heat until the edges just turn brown, about 1½–2 minutes, and flip to cook for another 30 seconds or so. Remove to a piece of wax paper and repeat with remaining batter, stacking the crepes.

Butternut Squash and Zucchini Crepes *(Vegetarian)*

Ricotta, caramelized onions, sage brown butter . . . I love the combination of savory and sweet in this crepe. The sweetness of the caramelized onions and the squash puree are a lovely combination.

Makes 12 crepes

1 whole butternut squash
2 sweet onions
1 medium zucchini
1 tablespoon extra-virgin olive oil
15 ounces ricotta cheese
1 cup cottage cheese
4 ounces cream cheese
1 egg yolk

½ teaspoon salt

1 stick butter

2 large sage leaves

1 batch **Basic Savory Crepes** *(see page 54)*

freshly ground black pepper

1. Heat the stick of butter in a small sauté pan over low heat with sage leaves until the butter just starts to brown (it will first bubble, then brown), about 10 minutes, removing the sage leaves after about 5 minutes. Strain through a fine-mesh sieve. Add to clean saucepan and set aside covered to keep warm until ready to use.

2. Preheat the oven to 325 degrees.

3. Halve and seed the squash and roast until soft, about 45–55 minutes. Once cooled slightly, remove the skin.

4. While the squash is roasting, slice the onions and dice the zucchini. Sauté in olive oil until lightly browned and soft, about 10–12 minutes

5. Put the squash, ricotta, cottage cheese, cream cheese, egg yolk, and salt in food processor and mix until very smooth.

6. Place 2 tablespoons of the filling in the center of each crepe. Add 1 tablespoon of the zucchini and onion mixture and fold in each side, creating small square envelopes. Place seam side down onto a parchment-lined rimmed baking sheet and repeat with all crepes.

7. In a large nonstick saute pan, brown the crepes, seam side down, in 3 tablespoons of the brown butter, until golden on both sides. Once browned, place on a lined cookie sheet and heat in the oven for 15 minutes.

8. To serve, place two crepes on a plate and drizzle with the browned butter. Add a few grinds of freshly cracked black pepper to taste.

Asparagus, Parmesan, *and* Ricotta Crepes Topped *with* Fresh Crab

This is my version of Crepes Oscar and a delicious way to enjoy Maine crab in its simplest form, without overpowering the delicate flavor of the crab.

Makes 12 crepes

18 asparagus stems, cut in half

15 ounces ricotta cheese

1 cup cottage cheese

1 egg yolk

½ teaspoon salt

1 cup grated Parmesan cheese

1 batch Basic Savory Crepes *(see page 54)*

½ cup shredded Parmesan cheese

1 stick butter

8 ounces fresh, cooked crab meat

lemon, for garnish

1. Heat the stick of butter in a small sauté pan over low heat until the butter just starts to brown (it will first bubble, then brown), about 10 minutes. Strain through a fine-mesh sieve. Add to clean saucepan and set aside covered to keep warm until ready to use.

2. Preheat the oven to 325 degrees.

3. Steam the asparagus in a microwave for 2 minutes.

4. Put the ricotta, cottage cheese, egg yolk, salt, and grated Parmesan in a food processor and mix until very smooth.

5. Place 2 tablespoons of filling in the center of each crepe. Add 3 pieces of asparagus and 1 tablespoon shredded Parmesan and tightly roll crepes. Place all crepes seam side down onto a parchment-lined rimmed baking sheet until ready to pan fry.

6. In a large nonstick saute pan, brown the crepes, seam

side down, in 3 tablespoons of the brown butter, until golden on both sides. Once browned, place on a lined cookie sheet and heat in the oven for 15 minutes.

7. Add the crab meat to the browned butter and stir to warm over low heat, about 2 minutes.

8. To serve, place two crepes on a plate, top with the crab meat, and drizzle with the browned butter and a squeeze of lemon.

Fried Eggs on Mushroom Hash
with Melted Swiss

This dish really can't get much easier or fresher. It's gluten-free and very satisfying. Throw some potatoes in the hash for a heartier dish.

Serves 4

2 tablespoons extra-virgin olive oil

4 tablespoons unsalted butter, divided

4 cups of a variety of mushrooms (shiitake, chanterelles, and morels are my favorites), roughly chopped

1 large bunch scallions (trimmed 1 inch from top and bottom), using both white and green parts, sliced ⅛–¼ inch thick

2 cups shredded Swiss cheese (you could substitute sharp cheddar or Monterey Jack)

8 large eggs

½ teaspoon paprika

salt, to taste

freshly ground black pepper, to taste

1. Preheat the oven to warm, about 175–190 degrees.

2. In a large sauté pan over medium heat, add the olive oil and 3 tablespoons of the butter. Add the mushrooms and half of the scallions and sauté until soft, about 10 minutes. Add the remaining scallions and top with the cheese. Cover and lower heat to a very low simmer for 5 minutes. Remove and place in warm oven until ready to plate.

3. Using a 12–14-inch frying pan, add the remaining 1 tablespoon of butter. When melted, crack the eggs one at a time into the pan and fry each to the desired level of doneness. Keep in warm oven, covered, until all eggs are cooked. If you don't have a large frying pan, use two smaller ones and cook 4 eggs in each pan.

4. Divide the mushroom mixture among the plates, top each with two fried eggs, then sprinkle with paprika, salt, and pepper.

Wild Mushroom *and* Brie Pan-Fried Crepes Topped *with* an Olive Oil Fried Egg *(Vegetarian)*

Earthy, buttery sautéed mushrooms and creamy brie are a wonderful combination. The truffle oil for me is the icing on the cake!

Serves 4

2 large shallots

½ stick butter, divided

2 cups mixed wild mushrooms

thyme leaves stripped from 2 sprigs

salt, to taste

pepper, to taste

4 Basic Savory Crepes *(see page 54)*

small wheel of brie (4 inches round), thinly sliced into 8 pieces

olive oil, for frying eggs

4 eggs

microgreens

truffle oil, to taste

chives, finely minced

1. Sauté shallots in 2 tablespoons of butter until lightly golden, 6–8 minutes. Add mushrooms and thyme leaves and sauté until browned, another 5-6 minutes. Add salt and pepper to taste.

2. Place 2 slices of brie in the center of each crepe, top with 2 tablespoons of the mushroom mixture, and fold in each side, creating small rectangular pouches. Place seam side down onto a parchment-lined, rimmed baking sheet.

3. In a large frying pan, melt remaining butter over medium heat and place each crepe, seam side down, and brown on both sides, about 3 minutes per side. Transfer to plate.

4. In the same pan, add eggs and fry over medium-high heat until edges are lightly browned and egg white is set.

5. Place crepe, seam side down, on a plate atop some microgreens. Top with a fried egg and a few mushrooms. Drizzle with truffle oil and garnish with chives.

Pan-Fried Crepes *with* Braised Asian Duck Topped *with* Fried Egg, Hoisin Butter, *and* Scallions

I appreciate creative Asian fusion in any meal. This is my twist on Peking Duck for breakfast. Make extra hoisin butter; it's delicious and offers a bit of that sweet and savory appeal, as you might notice throughout my recipes that I'm quite fond of!

Makes 4 crepes

32 ounces chicken stock

2 garlic cloves

1 (2-inch) piece of ginger

1 tablespoon fish sauce

1 tablespoon hoisin

¼ cup rice wine

2 duck legs

½ stick butter

4 large eggs

olive oil, for frying eggs

4 Basic Savory Crepes *(see page 54)*

salt, to taste

scallions, for garnish

shaved radishes, for garnish

1. In a heavy, deep saucepan, add chicken stock, garlic, ginger, fish sauce, hoisin, and rice wine and bring to boil. Reduce heat to medium-low and add duck legs. Cook until duck is tender enough to shred, about 2 hours. Remove duck and set on a plate.

2. Reduce stock until thickened. In small saucepan, add butter and ½ cup of reduced sauce and warm over low heat until well combined. Turn off heat and keep covered.

3. In a small sauté pan, fry eggs in 1 tablespoon of olive oil until edges are browned and whites are set.

4. While sauce is reducing, shred duck. Place crepes on the countertop and add about ¼ cup of shredded duck in the middle from just shy of edge to edge. Roll up and place seam side down on plates. Top with a fried egg, some shredded duck, and a spoonful of sauce. Garnish with sliced scallions and shaved radishes.

Buttermilk Fried Chicken *and* Malted Waffles *with* Maple Sriracha Syrup

If you haven't tried this sweet and savory combination, you should. For years I wondered what all the hype was about until I tried it. For me, the kicker is the maple sriracha syrup that ties it together so perfectly! You just might find a number of dishes to enjoy it with.

Serves 6; makes 12 (4-inch, square or quarters) Belgian-style waffles

Waffles

2¼ cups flour

2 tablespoons granulated sugar

⅛ teaspoon salt

½ cup vegetable oil

1½ cups 2% milk

1 large egg

¼ cup malted milk powder (found in baking supply stores)

2 tablespoons baking powder

To make the waffles:

In a large bowl, add all ingredients and mix with a whisk until well combined. Do not overmix—it's okay if the batter is slightly lumpy. Heat a waffle iron and coat with cooking spray. Ladle the batter into the iron and cook until golden brown and crispy, about 8 minutes (often longer than the manufacturer recommends).

Dana's Tip
Roasted, buttery Brussels sprouts make a great side for this dish.

Sriracha Maple Syrup

2 cups maple syrup
¼ cup sriracha

To make the sriracha maple syrup:

Add the maple syrup and sriracha in a bowl and whisk to combine.

Honey Butter

2 sticks softened butter
½ teaspoon salt
¼ teaspoon cracked pepper
pinch of cayenne
2 tablespoons honey
1 tablespoon confectioner sugar

To make the honey butter:

Using a stand mixer with a paddle attachment, blend all ingredients until smooth and fluffy.

Buttermilk Fried Chicken

4 boneless and skinless chicken breasts, cut into 1-inch-wide strips
1 cup buttermilk
⅛ cup sriracha
½ cup corn flour
1½ cups all-purpose flour
1½ teaspoons salt
1½ teaspoons garlic powder
1 teaspoon onion powder
¼ teaspoon dried oregano

¼ teaspoon dried thyme

1 teaspoon paprika

vegetable oil for frying

¼ teaspoon salt

½ teaspoon freshly ground black pepper

To make the fried chicken:

1. Combine the chicken, buttermilk, and sriracha in a large bowl and let soak at least 1 hour.

2. Mix together the corn flour, all-purpose flour, salt, garlic and onion powders, oregano, thyme, and paprika and set aside.

3. Heat 2 inches of oil in a heavy-bottomed pot to 350 degrees. Dredge the chicken in the flour mixture and fry in the oil until golden brown and cooked through, about 6–7 minutes. When the chicken comes out of hot oil, salt and pepper lightly.

To assemble the dish:

Place ½ waffle on a plate, then top with 3 fried chicken pieces, a scoop of honey butter, and a nice ladle of the sriracha maple syrup (with more on the side!).

Chive and Cheddar Waffles Topped *with* Fried Egg, Sriracha Butter, and Scallions *(Vegetarian)*

These cheesy, savory waffles are addictive. Imagine the flavor of a cheddar biscuit in waffle form!

Makes 6 waffles

2 cups all-purpose flour

2 teaspoons baking powder

½ teaspoon dry mustard

½ teaspoon paprika

3 tablespoons minced chives

1½ teaspoons kosher salt

½ teaspoon black pepper

2 large eggs

2 cups whole milk

1 stick unsalted butter, melted

2 cups shredded sharp cheddar cheese

3 tablespoons thinly sliced scallions, for garnish

1. Heat the oven to 250 degrees and position a rack in the middle. Set a wire rack on a baking sheet and place it in the oven.

2. Whisk together the flour, baking powder, mustard, paprika, chives, salt, and pepper in a large bowl and set aside.

3. Place the eggs in another large bowl and whisk until just broken up. Add the milk, and while whisking, slowly add the melted butter until combined. Fold in the cheese.

4. Add the milk and cheese mixture to the flour mixture and stir with a rubber spatula until the flour is just incorporated and no streaks remain (the batter may have a few lumps; you don't want to overmix). Set aside.

5. Heat a Belgian waffle iron to medium-high for at least 5 minutes. Coat with cooking spray, fill with batter, and cook until the steam stops coming from the waffle iron (open the top and check to see if the waffle is golden brown after 6–8 minutes, as all waffle irons cook differently). Transfer the waffle to the wire rack in the oven to keep warm. Repeat with the remaining batter.

Sriracha Butter

Makes enough for 6 waffles

2 sticks of butter
3 tablespoons sriracha
1 teaspoon salt
2 tablespoons honey

To make the sriracha butter:

Add all ingredients in a small
saucepan to melt and keep warm.

Eggs

6 large eggs
1 tablespoon olive oil
salt, to taste
pepper, to taste

To cook the eggs:

Fry the eggs in the olive oil over
medium heat until the edges
are crispy, the whites are done,
and the yolk is medium to soft.
Sprinkle salt and pepper on top.

To assemble the dish:

Place the waffle on a plate, halved, stacked at an angle to one another, then top with
the egg, drizzle the warm sriracha butter, and sprinkle with scallions.

Dana's Tip

*Placing the waffles on a wire rack and not directly on the sheet pan
allows air to circulate around the waffles so that they stay crispy.*

Lobster and Grits *with* Fried Egg *and* Smoked Tomato Butter *with* Chorizo, Crispy Bacon, *and* Scallions

The inspiration for this dish came from a restaurant in New Orleans where I had the best grits I've ever eaten. Southern food and shellfish make for a nice pair, and I wanted to create a breakfast dish around it.

Serves 4

Lobster and Sausage

4 tablespoons olive oil

1 pound smoked andouille sausage, sliced ¼ inch thick on a bias

1 red bell pepper, chopped

1 yellow bell pepper, chopped

1 poblano pepper, chopped

1 large sweet onion, small dice

½ teaspoon salt, divided

¼ teaspoon black pepper

2 cloves garlic, minced on a zester

½ teaspoon garlic powder

½ teaspoon onion powder

½ teaspoon smoked paprika

½ teaspoon sweet paprika

¼ teaspoon oregano

¼ teaspoon thyme

¼ teaspoon black pepper

¼ teaspoon cayenne

chopped fresh parsley

meat from three 1¼-pound lobsters

1 bunch of scallions, thinly sliced

juice of ½ lemon

To prepare the lobster and sausage:

Heat the olive oil in a large skillet. Add the sausage and brown, then transfer to a plate, leaving all of the fat in the pan. Add the peppers, onions, and some salt and pepper and sauté over medium heat until tender and lightly browned, about 10–12 minutes. Add the seasoning spices, remaining salt, reserved sausage, and remaining ½ cup lobster stock to the skillet and reduce for a few minutes. Add the cooked lobster to the skillet and let warm for a few minutes while getting the dishes ready to plate.

Eggs

4 large eggs
1 tablespoon olive oil
salt, to taste
coarsely cracked pepper, to taste

To cook the eggs:

Heat olive oil in sauté pan over medium heat, and when hot, carefully crack each egg into the pan. Cook until edges are browned and whites are set, about 4 minutes. Top with salt and coarsely cracked black pepper to taste.

Lobster Stock

Makes about 4 cups

shells and heads from 3 cooked 1¼-pound lobsters
1 large carrot
2 onions
olive oil, drizzle
2 tablespoons vegetable oil
½ stick butter
3 tablespoons tomato paste
1 cup dry white wine
8 cups water
2 bay leaves
a few sprigs of thyme
black peppercorns

To make the lobster stock:

1. With back of a heavy knife, crush the lobster shells and heads. Chop carrot and onion roughly.

2. Heat oven to 375 degrees. Roast the lobster shells with the onions and carrots with a drizzle of olive oil for 30 minutes.

3. In an 8-quart heavy stockpot, heat the oil and butter over medium heat and add carrot, onion, tomato paste, and wine and simmer until most of wine is evaporated. Add the water, bay leaves, thyme sprigs and peppercorns and simmer until liquid is reduced to about 4 cups, about 1½ hours. Pour the stock through a fine sieve into a heat-proof bowl. Stock may be made 3 days ahead and keeps, frozen, for up to 3 months.

Grits

5 tablespoons unsalted butter, divided

1 large or 2 small jalapeños, finely diced

1 large shallot, finely diced

5 tablespoons butter, divided

2½ cups good quality lobster or shellfish stock (or half chicken/ half vegetable stock if preferred)

2½ cups heavy cream

1 cup grits

1½ cups sharp cheddar, shredded

kosher salt, to taste

cracked black pepper, to taste

To make the grits:

1. Sauté the jalapeño and shallot with 1 tablespoon of butter over medium heat until soft and lightly caramelized, about 10–12 minutes.

2. Bring 2 cups of the lobster stock, heavy cream, and 4 tablespoons of butter to a simmer in a heavy saucepan. Gradually whisk in the grits. Reduce the heat and simmer until the grits have thickened, 15–20 minutes, stirring occasionally to avoid lumps. Once the grits are thick and creamy, adjust the consistency with stock or more cream, if necessary, then add the sautéed jalapeños and the cheese and mix until combined and melted. Season with salt and pepper to taste.

Dana's Tip

If you don't want to make your own lobster stock, "Better Than Boullion" brand makes a very good base that you can use instead, or you can add it to chicken or vegetable stock.

Smoked Tomato Butter Sauce

Makes about 2 cups

10 fresh plum tomatoes

1 can (28 oz.) San Marzano tomatoes

2 tablespoons olive oil

1 large sweet onion, finely chopped

kosher salt, to taste

pinch red pepper flakes

3 cloves garlic

2 tablespoons sugar

1 teaspoon smoked paprika

½ stick butter

2 tablespoons flat leaf parsley

To make the smoked tomato butter sauce:

1. Smoke the fresh tomatoes in a stovetop smoker: Cut the core of the tomatoes with a paring knife, then cut the tomatoes in half through the core end. Line the tomato halves cut side up on the smoking rack. Line the bottom pan with foil to catch the juices. Season the cut side of the tomatoes with salt and pepper. Smoke the tomatoes until they are softened and have a golden hue, about 35–40 minutes over the heat after closing the smoker lid. Then turn off the heat and let sit another 10 minutes with the smoker lid closed.

2. Cool the tomatoes a few minutes and set aside.

3. Heat the olive oil in a heavy saucepan over medium heat. Add the onion, season lightly with salt, and add the red pepper flakes. Continue to cook, stirring occasionally, until the onion is lightly browned, about 15 minutes. Stir in the garlic and cook about 2 minutes. Add both the smoked and canned tomatoes to the pan, lower the heat, add the sugar and paprika, and cook another 5 minutes. Add the sauce to a blender (or use an immersion blender) and puree until smooth. Add the butter and parsley and season to taste. For a smoother sauce, push through a fine-mesh sieve.

To assemble the dish:

Add the grits to a serving dish and top with the sausage and onion/pepper mixture. Add the scallions and a squeeze of lemon juice, then top with some lobster and smoked tomato butter. Garnish with parsley.

Vegetarian Stir Fry *with* Seared Tofu, Vegetables, *and* Sesame Soy Glaze

With kale, onions, wild mushrooms, edamame, sweet potatoes, and crispy fried wontons

This delicious vegetarian dish can be made vegan by substituting tortillas for the wontons and can be made gluten-free by using corn tortillas.

Serves 4

12–14 ounces extra-firm tofu

1 quart vegetable oil

8 wonton wrappers, cut on the diagonal

3 tablespoons light olive oil

1 large red onion

4 cups curly kale, torn

1½ cups wild mushrooms

1 zucchini, cut into 1-inch cubes

1 large garlic clove, finely minced

1 teaspoon fresh grated ginger

1 large sweet potato, peeled and cut into 1-inch cubes

¼ cup cooked edamame

2 tablespoons soy sauce

1 teaspoon sesame oil

a few grinds of coarse cracked black pepper

salt, to taste

Chive Oil, for garnish *(see page 190)*

1. Place tofu on a plate. Set a plate on top and weight it down with a heavy canned food item or two. Let tofu drain for 30 minutes, then pat dry.

2. Heat vegetable oil in a 2- to 3-quart sauce pan. When hot, add wontons and fry until golden brown on both sides, about 30–45 seconds per side. Remove to paper towel and salt to taste.

3. In a separate large frying pan, add 1 tablespoon olive oil and sauté tofu over medium-high heat until browned on all sides, about 10–12 minutes. Set aside in a large bowl. Add another tablespoon olive oil to the pan and sauté onion over medium-high heat until edges brown, about 10 minutes. Add kale and continue to

cook 5 minutes. Remove onions and kale to the bowl with the tofu. Add mushrooms and zucchini to pan and sauté for about 8 minutes over medium-high heat. Add garlic and ginger and cook 1 minute longer. Add the cooked mushrooms and zucchini to the same bowl. Add another tablespoon of olive oil and sauté sweet potatoes over medium-high heat until tender and lightly browned, about 15 minutes. Then add all cooked vegetables to the pan, and add soy sauce, sesame oil, and cracked black pepper. Mix all ingredients until warmed through. Salt to taste. Serve with fried wonton wedges and a drizzle of chive oil.

Garlic Sausage, Chorizo, *and* Vegetable Stir Fry *with* an Olive Oil Fried Egg

With spinach, peppers, red onion, corn, scallions, fried flour tortillas, and sriracha sour cream

This stir fry can be made gluten-free by substituting corn tortillas for flour tortillas.

Serves 4

2 tablespoons sriracha

½ cup sour cream

1 teaspoon salt, divided

olive oil, for sautéing

8 ounces sweet Italian or garlic sausage, no casings or casings removed

1 large red onion, cut into ½-inch slices

1 each red and orange bell peppers, diced

2 links chorizo sausage, cut into a small dice

1 large ear of fresh corn, cut from the cob

1 large garlic clove, minced

6 cups fresh baby spinach

4 large eggs

2 flour tortillas

salt, to taste

a few grinds of freshly cracked black pepper, to taste

1 bunch of scallions, thinly sliced

cilantro, chopped (optional) to taste

1. In small bowl, mix sriracha, sour cream, and salt until well blended. Set aside.

2. In large sauté pan, add 1 tablespoon olive oil and Italian sausage and cook until lightly browned. Remove to a small bowl. To same pan, add onions and peppers and cook over medium-high heat until vegetables are softened and lightly charred, about 10–12 minutes. Add diced chorizo and the corn and cook for 5 minutes. Add the garlic and baby spinach and continue to cook until spinach is wilted. Add ½ teaspoon salt, or to taste. Lower heat and simmer, covered, until eggs are ready.

3. In another large frying pan, add 1 tablespoon olive oil, and when hot, add eggs and cook until edges are lightly browned and crispy and whites are set, about 4 minutes. Salt and pepper to taste.

4. To plate, divide the sausage and vegetable mixture among the plates. Top with fried egg, a drizzle of sriracha cream, sliced scallions, and cilantro (optional).

Creamy Spinach *and* Artichokes *with* a Fried Egg on Crostini

A really good spinach and artichoke dip with crusty bread could easily be my last meal! Here it makes a nice accompaniment to a fried egg.

Serves 4

1 loaf ciabatta, sliced ¼-inch thick

1 shallot, finely diced

3 tablespoons butter

2 cloves of garlic, minced

9–10 ounces frozen artichokes, thawed and roughly chopped

1 10-ounce bag fresh baby spinach

½ teaspoon salt

2 ounces cream cheese

2 tablespoons sour cream

2 tablespoons mayonnaise

¼ cup heavy cream

4 ounces fresh mozzarella, diced

4 ounces shredded Parmesan cheese

½ teaspoon coarse black pepper

2 tablespoons olive oil

4 large eggs

½ teaspoon salt, to taste

microgreens, for garnish

tri-color bell peppers, finely diced, for garnish

1. Toast sliced ciabatta in a 350-degree oven until lightly browned. Set aside.

2. Sauté shallot in 1½ tablespoons butter over medium heat until lightly browned, about 8–10 minutes. Add the garlic and cook another minute. Add artichokes and spinach and cook until wilted and most of the water released from the spinach has evaporated. Add ½ teaspoon of salt or to taste. Turn off heat and add the cream cheese, sour cream, mayonnaise, and heavy cream and mix until incorporated. Add mixture to a large bowl and toss in mozzarella and Parmesan and mix thoroughly. Add some cracked black pepper and pour into baking dish. Bake until bubbly, about 20–25 minutes.

3. While spinach and artichoke mixture is baking, add olive oil and remaining 1½ tablespoons butter to a pan, and when hot, fry eggs until the edges are browned and crispy and whites are fully set. Lightly salt and pepper.

4. Top each crostini with a couple tablespoons (or more!) of the cheese and a fried egg. Garnish with microgreens and finely diced tri-color bell peppers.

Sausage *and* Scrambled Egg Soft Tacos

*With cheddar, scallions, sliced avocado, lime, avocado crema,
salsa fresca, and smoked paprika oil*

Substitute corn tortillas for flour to make this gluten-free.

Serves 4

6 ounces garlic or sweet Italian sausage, no casings or casings removed
¼ teaspoon smoked paprika
½ teaspoon chipotle powder
2 tablespoons butter, divided
1 shallot, diced
8 large eggs
½ teaspoon salt, divided
¼ cup heavy cream
¼ cup cheddar cheese
¼ cup Monterey Jack cheese
8 flour or corn tortillas
1 bunch scallions, thinly sliced

1. In a frying pan, add sausage, smoked
   paprika and chipotle chile powder
   and cook over medium heat for 6-7
   minutes. Add 1 tablespoon butter,
   ¼ teaspoon salt and diced shallot
   and sauté another 4-5 minutes,
   until shallot is softened and lightly
   browned. Remove to plate, cover
   and keep warm in very low oven.

2. Beat eggs with cream, ¼ teaspoon
   salt and heavy cream until well
   combined.

3. In same pan the sausage and
   shallots were cooked in, add 1
   tablespoon butter and scramble the
   eggs until just soft. Fold in cheddar.

Avocado Crema

2 ripe avocados
½ cup sour cream
½ teaspoon salt, plus some to taste
½ teaspoon ancho chile powder
1 lime
black pepper to taste

Mash 1 avocado with the sour cream, ½ teaspoon salt, chile powder, the juice from half of the lime and mix until well combined. If you want a very smooth crema, mix using a blender. Let sit for a couple of hours for flavors to meld. Add black pepper and salt, or to taste.

Salsa Fresca

1 medium tomato
1 tablespoon red onion
1 small jalapeño
½ teaspoon sugar

Finely dice the tomato, red onion, and jalapeno and blend with the juice from the other lime half, ¼ teaspoon of salt and ½ teaspoon of sugar. Let sit for a couple of hours for flavors to meld.

Smoked Paprika Oil *(see page 191)*
avocado slices, for garnish

To assemble, divide the eggs among 8 tortillas. Top with the sausage mixture, some avocado crema, and salsa fresca. Garnish with sliced avocado and sliced scallions. Drizzle smoked paprika oil over the top.

Grilled Pork Tenderloin Breakfast Cubano

With fried egg, bacon, Swiss, creamy Dijon, and cornichon,
on griddled English muffin

Serves 4 (with enough pork remaining for leftovers)

4 slices of thick-cut bacon

1 tablespoon Dijon mustard

1 tablespoon mayonnaise

1 small pork tenderloin, about 1½ pounds

Pork Marinade *(see recipe below)*

1 tablespoon olive oil

4 large eggs

salt and pepper, to taste

4 English muffins, lightly toasted

8 cornichon (or other tart baby dill pickle), split lengthwise or chopped

4 slices of imported Swiss

1. Cook bacon on a sheet pan at 350 degrees until crispy, about 20 minutes. Remove to drain on a towel. Cut each piece in half.

2. Mix Dijon mustard and mayonnaise and set aside.

3. Combine all marinade ingredients and marinate pork for 3–4 hours. Grill on a gas or charcoal grill until thermometer reads 145–150 degrees. Remove tenderloin to a plate and cover. It will continue to cook once removed from the grill. Let cool. With a sharp knife, cut into very thin slices.

4. Heat olive oil in a sauté pan and when hot, add the eggs. Fry eggs for 2 minutes, then flip and cook another 2 minutes. The yolk should be only slightly soft; otherwise it's a delicious but messier sandwich! Lightly salt and pepper.

5. To assemble, spread some of the Dijon mixture onto each muffin half. Top each half with 2 half slices of bacon and about 6 slices of pork, depending on how thin you've cut them. Top with sliced cornichon and a piece of Swiss. Put bottom half under broiler until cheese is just melted. Top with a fried egg and enjoy.

Pork Marinade

1 tablespoon soy sauce	½ teaspoon garlic powder
1 tablespoon olive oil	½ teaspoon onion powder
1 tablespoon brown sugar	½ teaspoon black pepper
1 teaspoon smoked paprika	

The Royal Crustacean

Classic Crab Imperial on a toasted English muffin with melted Havarti, a brown butter fried egg, a touch of mayo, and Old Bay seasoning

My friend Michele from Maryland (whom I met when she stayed with us at the Kingsleigh Inn many times) hooked me up with Duke Marshall, who owns Drum Point Market on Smith Island in Chesapeake Bay. Although I love Maine crab, there just isn't anything like jumbo lump crab from the Maryland blue crab. I ordered enough to last us many, many months. I made Crab Imperial for dinner the night the crab arrived. But because we ate about a half a pound just out of the container (as Duke said we wouldn't be able to resist), we couldn't finish dinner! So I had leftovers. What to do with it in the morning for breakfast? Incorporate into scrambled eggs? No, I wanted something different. And so, based on the Cubano breakfast recipe I love so much, this breakfast sandwich was born!

Serves 4

Crab Imperial

½ cup mayonnaise

1½ teaspoons Worcestershire

1 tablespoon lemon juice

1 tablespoon capers

1½ teaspoons Dijon mustard

½ teaspoon salt

1 pound jumbo lump crab meat

¼ teaspoon Old Bay seasoning

paprika, for dusting

Mix mayonnaise, Worcestershire, lemon juice, capers, Dijon, and salt. Carefully fold in crab, then top with paprika. Bake in a small ramekin or baking dish at 350 degrees for about 25 minutes, but no longer or the sauce will "break," which means it will become translucent and buttery rather than creamy. (This is not so bad if it happens, however, and will not affect flavor.) Keep covered for a few minutes until you are ready to assemble the dish.

1 tablespoon brown butter for frying eggs *(see recipe below)*

4 large eggs

4 English muffins

1 tablespoon mayonnaise, for English muffin

4 slices of creamy Havarti (to fit the size of the English muffin)

Old Bay, for dusting

1 stick of butter

To make browned butter: In small saucepan, add 1 stick of butter and cook over medium-low heat until lightly brown in color and milk solids have fully separated, about 8–10 minutes, watching very carefully not to burn the butter. Strain through fine-mesh sieve and set aside until ready to use.

Meanwhile, add 1 tablespoon brown butter to a frying pan and fry eggs until yolk is medium hard, about 2 minutes per side.

To assemble:

Toast English muffins and spread a small amount of mayonnaise on just the top half. Place a slice of Havarti on the top half and broil until cheese is melted and only lightly golden and bubbling. Then place about ¼–½ cup of the warm Crab Imperial on the bottom half of the toasted muffin. The butter from the crab will seep in and flavor it nicely.

Place egg on top of the crab side of the muffin, dust with some Old Bay and then cover with the cheese side of the muffin. You will need a couple napkins!

Dana's Tip

Brown butter is simply clarified butter (also known as ghee) that has been browned to create a nutty, rich flavor. It can sit at room temperature in an airtight container, though depending on how cool your house is, it might solidify.

POACHED EGGS ON
POTATO, ONION, AND
BACON HASH, *page 88*

CHAPTER 4

Beyond the Benedict—Poached Egg Creations

You won't find an English muffin or slice of Canadian bacon here. You will find some delicious and creative poached egg combinations with lots of flavor and balance of textures.

Poached Eggs on Potato, Onion, *and* Bacon Hash
With grated sharp cheddar, truffled sour cream,
and fresh chives

This is my breakfast version of a loaded baked potato! Delicious for brunch or light dinner with a salad. And it's gluten-free.

Serves 4

1 cup sour cream

1 teaspoon white truffle oil (I use Fiore from Maine)

½ teaspoon salt

1 tablespoon fresh chopped chives, plus more for garnish

4 strips thick-cut (hardwood smoked) bacon, diced

2 tablespoons extra-virgin olive oil

1 large Vidalia (or sweet) onion, diced

3 large Yukon Gold potatoes, cubed

½ teaspoon paprika

1 cup shredded sharp white cheddar cheese, plus more for garnish

¼ cup white vinegar

8 large eggs

1 10-ounce package of fresh baby spinach

1. Preheat the oven to 250 degrees.

2. In a small bowl, mix together the sour cream, truffle oil, salt, and chives and set aside.

3. In a large sauté pan, cook the bacon over medium heat until crisp, about 10–12 minutes, and remove with a slotted spoon. Set aside. To the same pan add the olive oil and sauté the onions and potatoes until tender and the onions are lightly caramelized, about 15–18 minutes. Add the paprika, toss in the bacon, top with shredded cheddar, and keep covered in the oven until poached eggs are ready.

Dana's Tip

If you're wanting to serve a larger crowd and don't know how to manage poaching that many eggs, either to order or to remain warm and not overcooked, poach them 3 minutes and place them in a bowl of ice water. When ready to serve, simply warm them as you need to, in a pan of clean simmering water for about 2 minutes and you'll have a perfectly poached egg. I've successfully poached 100 eggs this way!

Poaching the Eggs

1. Fill a 2- to 3-quart sauce pan three-fourths the way up with water and add the white vinegar. Bring to a slow rolling boil.

2. Crack one egg into a small dish or ramekin and lower the very edge of the dish into the boiling water, allowing some water to enter the dish, so the egg falls gently into the water. Repeat with the remaining eggs. Cook for 3–4 minutes for a softer yolk. To hold warm if not immediately ready to serve, remove the eggs after 3 minutes and place them in bowl of warm water to keep warm for a couple minutes until you can serve all at once. If you aren't ready to serve for a longer period of time, place the eggs into ice water instead of warm water and then when ready to serve, place them into very low simmering water for 2–3 minutes to rewarm.

3. When ready to serve, remove the eggs from the warm water with a slotted spoon and place on a paper towel to absorb any water before plating. Wet poached eggs aren't a good thing!

To plate, put a small amount of baby spinach on each plate. Top with the potato hash, 2 poached eggs, and a tablespoon or two of the sour cream mixture. Garnish with fresh chopped chives and some additional shredded cheddar if you'd like.

Poached Eggs over Sweet Potato Latkes Topped *with* Caramelized Shallots *and* Poblano Cream Sauce

Lori Lynn, a favorite inn guest of ours from Texas, sat at the breakfast table one morning and said, "That sauce is so good I could bathe in it!" Imagine in that fun Texas accent. That was a line I won't soon forget!

Serves 4

2 tablespoons extra-virgin olive oil

1 large sweet onion, diced

1 large poblano pepper, seeds and ribs removed and cut into a very small dice

1 cup heavy cream

salt, to taste

1 pint sour cream

1 lemon, halved

 ground black pepper, to taste

8 large eggs, poached *(see page 89)*

3 tablespoons fresh chopped chives

1 10-ounce package of fresh baby spinach

8 Sweet Potato Latkes *(see recipe below)*

1. Heat the olive oil in a pan and sauté the onions and pepper until soft and lightly caramelized. Add heavy cream, salt, and pepper to taste, and reduce until thickened. Keep covered over very low simmer while poaching eggs. Once eggs are just about done, add sour cream and the juice from one lemon half into the sauce that has been simmering. Heat until just combined, a couple minutes. Add salt, pepper, and more lemon to taste.

To serve, place 2 small (about 4-inch) sweet potato latkes *(see page 174)* per plate over fresh baby spinach. Add a poached egg atop each latke and top with a couple of tablespoons of the cream sauce (or more, if you're like me!).

Poached Eggs in a Roasted Heirloom Tomato *with* Goat Cheese

I like to serve this with toasted ciabatta or focaccia bread for dipping.

Serves 4

4 medium-sized ripe heirloom tomatoes, halved

4 tablespoons extra-virgin olive oil

1 tablespoon granulated sugar

salt, to taste

freshly ground black pepper, to taste

8 large eggs

8 ounces goat cheese

1 10-ounce package of fresh baby spinach

2 tablespoons fresh chopped chives, for garnish

paprika, for garnish

Poached Eggs *(see page 89)*

1. Preheat the oven to 350 degrees.

2. Place the tomato halves on a baking sheet, cut side up. Scoop a very small amount of the center out with a small 1-1½-inch cookie scoop. Drizzle with olive oil, sugar, and salt and pepper to taste, and roast for about 45 minutes.

To plate, place a heaping tablespoon of goat cheese on each tomato. Top it with a poached egg and place it over a bed of baby spinach. Garnish with the chopped chives, some more cracked pepper, and a dash of paprika.

Crispy Potato Latke, Smoked Salmon, Brie, *and* Poached Egg

With lemon cream, fresh dill, red onion, capers, chives, and lemon thyme breadcrumbs (and caviar option)

I served this at a Cellardoor Winery seven-course brunch event for forty, and it was a big hit! The lemon cream and lemon thyme breadcrumbs add a nice element. And because you can prepare the latkes in advance and rewarm, it's a simple dish to put together for entertaining.

Serves 8

8 large eggs, poached *(see page 89)*

8 Classic Potato Latkes *(see recipe below)*

1 10-ounce package fresh baby spinach

8 ounces thinly sliced smoked salmon

8 slices of good quality brie, cut into ¼-inch × 2-inch slices or wedges

2 tablespoons capers

2 tablespoons red onion, finely diced

2 tablespoons fresh dill, minced

1 lemon, juice and zest separated

1½ teaspoons kosher salt, divided

¼ teaspoon coarse cracked pepper

kosher salt and fresh cracked pepper, for dusting over top finished dish

Crispy Lemon Thyme Breadcrumbs *(see recipe below)*

Lemon Crème Fraiche *(see recipe below)*

Crispy Lemon Thyme Breadcrumbs

1 standard baguette (about 10-12 inches)

¼ stick butter, melted

zest from 1 lemon

salt, pinch

4 thyme sprigs, leaves stripped

1. Prepare the crispy lemon thyme breadcrumbs by pulsing the baguette in a food processor until you have very coarse crumbs.

2. Add melted butter, lemon zest, a pinch of salt, and thyme and mix just to combine, ending up with crumbs that resemble panko in size.

3. Toast on sheet pan at 325 degrees until golden and fragrant, about 15 minutes. Alternatively, tossing panko crumbs with the butter, lemon zest, and thyme and toasting works well. (Bread crumbs freeze really well, too.)

Lemon Crème Fraiche

½ cup sour cream

4 ounces mascarpone, softened

¼ cup heavy cream

1½ teaspoons Dijon

the juice from 1 lemon

¾ teaspoon salt

¼ teaspoon pepper

1. Prepare the lemon creme fraiche by blending the sour cream, mascarpone, heavy cream, Dijon mustard, lemon juice, ¾ teaspoon salt, and ¼ teaspoon pepper. Adjust salt to taste.

2. Store in squeeze bottle until ready to use. Keep refrigerator for up to 5 days.

To assemble:

Place a small handful of baby spinach on a plate. Add a potato latke, a slice of smoked salmon, and brie. Using a torch, burn the brie just so it melts slightly and the outside edges char. Then add a poached egg and a drizzle of the lemon crème fraiche. Top with red onion, capers, dill, and a scattering of lemon thyme breadcrumbs. Finish with a dusting of kosher salt and freshly cracked pepper.

Steakhouse Poached Eggs

With garlic butter crostini, thinly sliced filet mignon, poached egg, creamed spinach hollandaise, and minced chives

This is one of my personal favorites; I came up with it for a Stonewall Kitchen class that remains on my class rotation. It's got all the classic elements of a steakhouse dinner brought together breakfast-style. Served with mimosas, it makes a great brunch or dinner, why not?

Serves 8

Garlic Butter Crostini

Yields about 12–14 slices

1 loaf of crusty Italian bread (about 4–5 inches in diameter)
1 stick butter
2 garlic cloves, minced
pinch of salt
freshly cracked pepper

To make the garlic butter crostini:

1. Preheat the oven to 375 degrees.

2. Slice the bread into ⅓-inch slices on a bias. In a small saucepan, melt butter with minced garlic, salt, and pepper and let heat over medium-low heat for 3 minutes, just to get rid of the very raw garlic taste. Spread the melted garlic butter on the bread and toast the bread in the oven until lightly browned but not hard-crisp, about 15 minutes.

Sliced Filet Mignon

Serves 8

tenderloin of beef, about 2–2½ pounds
2 teaspoons coarse sea salt
cracked black pepper
½ stick butter, softened

To prepare the filet mignon:

1. Let beef stand at room temperature 1 hour before roasting.
2. Position rack in center of the oven and preheat to 425 degrees.
3. Season beef with salt and a good amount of freshly cracked black pepper, pressing into the meat. Rub the roast with butter. Return the tenderloin to the rack on the baking sheet and roast until a thermometer inserted into thickest part of meat registers 125 degrees for medium-rare and 135–140 degrees in thinnest part, about 35 minutes. Remove roast from the oven and let rest 15 minutes before slicing.

Creamed Spinach Hollandaise

Makes enough to top 8 eggs

4 tablespoons butter, divided
1 clove garlic, minced
2 medium shallots, finely chopped
2 tablespoons all-purpose flour
1½ cups whole milk
¼ cup heavy cream
¼ cup grated Parmesan cheese
dash hot sauce
grated fresh nutmeg (a few passes on the zester)
1 tablespoon olive oil
10 ounces fresh spinach leaves (about 5 cups), roughly chopped

1 teaspoons lemon juice

kosher salt, to taste

freshly ground black pepper, to taste

To make the hollandaise:

1. Melt 2 tablespoons butter in a saucepan over medium heat. Add the garlic and shallots and cook, stirring, until just softened, about 3 minutes. Add flour and cook, stirring constantly, until the mixture just begins to brown and flour smells toasted, about 4 minutes. Whisking constantly, slowly stir in milk and cream until no lumps remain. Bring to a simmer and cook until thickened, about 5 minutes. Add Parmesan and hot sauce and stir until completely melted. Simmer over very low heat, stirring occasionally, for about 15 minutes. Add nutmeg.

2. While the creamy sauce mixture simmers, melt the remaining 2 tablespoons of butter with the olive oil in a small skillet over medium heat. Add baby spinach and cook, stirring, until completely wilted, about 3 minutes. Drain. Add to the sauce mixture and cook another 5 minutes. Add lemon juice, season with salt and pepper, and keep warm until ready to serve.

Garnish

1 pint of cherry tomatoes, halved

1 bunch of chives, minced

To assemble the dish:

Place one slice of crostini on the plate. Top with 2 or 3 thin slices of roasted filet, then one poached egg (*see page 89*), followed by a generous scoop of the creamed spinach. Top the plate with some chives and garnish with cherry tomato halves.

Corned Beef on Crispy Potato Latkes Topped *with* Poached Eggs, Whole-Grain Mustard Hollandaise, *and* Fried Shallots

This is one of my personal favorites. It's also great use of leftovers from a corned beef dinner. The sauce, while creamy, is lightened by the tart whole-grain mustard, reminiscent of the lemon in a classic Hollandaise. Top mine with extra, please!

Classic Potato Latkes *(see page 175)*
Poached Eggs *(see page 89)*

Corned Beef

Serves 8 to 10

1 5-pound cured corned brisket of beef

4 cloves garlic, smashed

2 bay leaves

1 tablespoon whole peppercorns

1 tablespoon whole allspice

1 tablespoon whole cloves

1 tablespoon mustard seeds

To make the corned beef:

1. Preheat the oven to 300 degrees.

2. Remove the corned beef from the brine, rinse thoroughly and set it fat side down in a heavy pot or Dutch oven. Cover with cold water and add the remaining ingredients. Over medium-high heat, bring the liquid almost to the point of boiling, then cover the pot and transfer it to the oven for 3½–4 hours or until very tender but not falling apart. You can also cook the meat on the stovetop, over a medium simmer for about 3½ hours or until tender.

3. When the meat is done (it will be fork tender), let it rest for a few minutes on a cutting board. Be sure to slice it against the grain, as this is a key step to the tender chew you should end up with.

Mustard Hollandaise

1 stick butter

1 cup heavy cream

1½ tablespoons coarse whole-grain mustard

1 tablespoon fresh chives, diced

½ teaspoon salt

freshly cracked black pepper, to taste

To make the hollandaise:

Combine the butter and cream in small saucepan and reduce until slightly thickened. Add mustard, chives, salt, and pepper to taste. Keep warm, covered, over very low heat until ready to plate.

Garnish

1 cup vegetable oil

4 shallots, thinly sliced

2 cups baby spinach

½ cup fresh chives, diced

To make the fried shallot garnish:

In a small saucepan, heat the oil to about 375 degrees and fry shallots until browned, about 2–3 minutes. Remove and drain on a paper towel.

To assemble the dish:

Place a small handful of spinach on a plate and top with potato latke (*see page 175*), a few slices of corned beef, 2 poached eggs (*see page 89*), a couple spoonfuls of the hollandaise, a scattering of fried shallots, and fresh chives.

Crispy Polenta, Prosciutto, Parmesan, *and* Poached Egg *with* Smoked Tomato Butter Sauce

Oh, this smoked tomato sauce is absolutely delicious and worth the effort! And because it freezes well, you can make a big batch and have more ready for the next time. It's gluten-free and vegetarian if you omit the prosciutto and substitute vegetable stock for the chicken stock.

Serves 6

Smoked Tomato Butter Sauce *(see page 73)*

Poached Eggs *(see page 89)*

Polenta

3 cups water

3 cups chicken stock

1 teaspoon salt

2 cups yellow cornmeal or polenta (not instant)

¾ stick butter

½ cup grated Parmesan cheese

½ teaspoon garlic powder

salt, to taste

pepper, to taste

2 tablespoons light olive oil

2 tablespoons butter

To make the polenta:

1. Add the water, chicken stock, and salt to a deep sauce pan and bring to a boil over high heat.

2. Once boiling, add the polenta while continuously whisking to prevent lumps. Turn the heat down to low and let simmer until thickened, 10–15 minutes.

3. Once thickened, stir in the butter, grated Parmesan, and garlic powder until smooth. Season with salt and pepper to taste. Spread the mixture into a greased baking dish or rimmed sheet pan lined with greased parchment and let cool in the refrigerator, uncovered, until solid.

4. Slice the polenta into your desired shape (with a biscuit cutter or just into squares, figuring each piece is a base for the poached egg). Add the oil and butter to a nonstick or cast-iron skillet and heat over medium heat. Once the oil is hot and glistening, but not smoking, add the polenta slices and cook until golden on each side. Add more oil as needed to fry the remaining slices. Keep warm in low oven until ready to plate.

Garnish

12 slices of prosciutto

6 cups baby arugula

microgreens, for topping

fresh coarsely cracked black pepper

4-ounce block of Parmesan cheese, shaved

12 basil leaves, minced

Chive Oil *(see page 190)*

To assemble the dish:

Place a cup of baby arugula on the plate. Add 2 slices of the seared polenta, top each with prosciutto, 2 poached eggs, and a couple of good-sized spoonfuls of the smoked tomato butter sauce (*see page 000*). Add a bit of microgreens and some cracked pepper, and then top the entire plate with shaved Parmesan and minced basil. Drizzle chive oil around the plate.

Dana's Tip

The smoked tomato butter sauce can dress up the simplest egg dish and is quite versatile. It freezes well too. Just leave room at the top of the squeeze bottle or container for expansion.

Poached Egg on Fried Green Tomatoes *with* Crispy Bacon, Seared Shrimp (or Lobster), and Creamy Spicy Remoulade

The fried green tomatoes alone make a great small plate or first course. Add the poached egg and shellfish, and you've got an elegant dish for brunch or lunch.

Serves 4

4 large eggs (for dredging)

2 tablespoons milk

2–3 large green tomatoes

¼ teaspoon kosher salt

½ cup flour, for dusting

vegetable oil, for frying

2 cups panko bread crumbs

4 slices thick-cut bacon, diced

12 ounces medium peeled, deveined raw shrimp (or 8 ounces of lobster, if using)

5 tablespoons butter

1 tablespoon olive oil

2 cups loosely packed baby greens (I like spinach or arugula)

8 eggs, poached *(see page 89)*

2 tablespoons fresh chives, diced

a small chunk of fresh Parmesan for shaving over the dish

Remoulade *(see recipe below)*

In a medium bowl, whisk 4 eggs with the milk and set aside for dredging the tomatoes.

To prepare the tomatoes:

1. Slice tomatoes into 3–4 equally thick slices, about ¼ inch. Lightly salt and dust with flour. Heat oil in large, deep pan to about 375 degrees. Dip each slice of floured tomato into the egg mixture, then into the panko breadcrumbs, pushing the crumbs onto the surface and coating completely. Add a few tomatoes at a time to the oil, but don't overcrowd. They'll take only 3–4 minutes. Remove and let sit on a paper towel. (You can keep them warm by then moving them to a dry sheet pan and placing in a 225-degree oven until ready to serve.)

2. Cook bacon until crisp, drain, and set aside.

3. Sauté peeled, deveined raw shrimp in 1 tablespoon olive oil with 2 tablespoons butter until pink and opaque, about 3 minutes per side. If using lobster, add 8 ounces of lobster to a small saucepan with 2 tablespoons of butter just to warm over low heat 3–4 minutes.

Remoulade

1 cup mayonnaise

2 tablespoons Dijon mustard

1 tablespoon horseradish

1 teaspoon pickle relish

1 tablespoon minced shallot

½ teaspoon fresh dill

1 teaspoon Worcestershire

1 teaspoon ketchup

1 teaspoon smoked paprika

½ teaspoon seafood seasoning

1 tablespoon fresh diced chives

¼ teaspoon salt

⅛ teaspoon cayenne

1 teaspoon fresh lemon juice

a few cracks of fresh ground black pepper

To make the remoulade:

Place all ingredients in blender and mix well. Place in squeeze bottle and let sit in the refrigerator at least an hour to allow flavors to meld.

To assemble the dish:

Place a small handful of baby greens, then top with 2 fried green tomatoes, then a poached egg. Drizzle remoulade and top with crumbled bacon and seared shrimp (or lobster). Garnish with a sprinkling of fresh chives and some shaved Parmesan.

POACHED EGG
ON FRIED GREEN
TOMATOES, *page 106*

POACHED EGG ON
CROSTINI, *page 110*

Poached Egg on Crostini *with* Baby Arugula, Tomato, Caramelized Onions, Cauliflower Truffle Cream, and Chives

Cauliflower bisque soup was my inspiration for this sauce. Crunchy crostini, creamy sauce, sweet caramelized onions, and the freshness of a tomato slice all complement a perfectly poached egg. It's a nice balance of textures and flavors.

Serves 8

1 stick butter, divided

1 medium sweet onion, diced

kosher salt, to taste

8 poached eggs *(see page 89)*

1 large loaf of ciabatta or crusty Italian bread

8 packed cups of baby arugula (or other baby greens)

2–3 ripe heirloom tomatoes (to yield 8 ¼-inch slices)

a chunk of Parmesan cheese, for shaving over the eggs

Cauliflower Truffle Cream *(see page 111)*

1 bunch of chives

Smoked Paprika Oil *(see page 191)*

freshly cracked black pepper, to taste

Preheat oven to 375 degrees.

Caramelize the onions:

1. In a large sauté pan over medium-high heat, add ½ stick of butter and when bubbling, add onions. Cook for 5 minutes, stirring regularly.

2. Then turn heat down to medium-low and continue to cook until golden brown, about 16–18 minutes. Once browned, salt to taste and just remove from burner. Keep covered until ready to plate.

Prepare the crostini:

1. Slice ciabatta into 8 ½- to ¾-inch slices and spread remaining butter among the slices.

2. Toast in oven until edges are golden, about 12–14 minutes. Set aside until ready to plate.

Cauliflower Truffle Cream

Makes about 3 cups

1 head cauliflower
½ stick plus 1 tablespoon unsalted butter
2 tablespoons light olive oil
1 large sweet onion, diced
2 cloves garlic, minced
2 cups chicken broth or stock
1 cup heavy cream
1 tablespoon white truffle oil
salt, to taste
freshly ground black pepper, to taste
diced fresh chives and a drizzle of truffle oil, for garnish

To make the cauliflower truffle cream:

1. Remove leaves and core from the cauliflower, roughly cut into small pieces, and put on baking sheet with ½ stick butter, cut into pieces, and roast until tender, about 30 minutes.

2. Heat olive oil and remaining tablespoon of butter in a large sauce pan or stockpot over medium heat. Add onion and cook until soft and lightly browned, about 10 minutes. Add the garlic and cook another 2 minutes. Then add the cooked cauliflower and sauté for 5 minutes. Add the stock and cream and bring to a boil. Reduce the heat to a simmer and cook until the cauliflower has had a chance to meld with the ingredients, about 10 minutes.

3. Remove from heat. Blend with an immersion blender (or in a blender) and puree the sauce until very smooth. At this point, you could push through a fine-mesh sieve for a velvety smooth sauce, but it isn't crucial. Add the truffle oil and salt and pepper to taste. Keep warm until ready to plate.

To assemble the dish:

Place a slice of the toasted crostini on a plate, top with some baby arugula, a slice of tomato sprinkled with salt, a poached egg, and a couple spoonfuls of cauliflower sauce. Sprinkle some chives over top and drizzle smoked paprika oil around the plate. Add more truffle oil on top, to taste.

Crispy Loaded Tortilla Topped *with* a Poached Egg

With shredded cheddar, black beans, caramelized onions, poblano peppers, crumbled sausage, smoked tomato butter sauce, and avocado

This is the kitchen sink tortilla! Loads of toppings on a crispy pan-fried tortilla topped off with a poached egg. And don't skip getting a good caramelization on the poblanos and onions; they lend so much flavor. Leave out the sausage and it's vegetarian; use corn tortillas to make it gluten-free.

Serves 4

1½ tablespoons olive oil, divided

4 flour or corn tortillas

8 ounces sweet or spicy sausage, casings removed

1 medium onion, finely diced

1 poblano pepper, finely diced

1 cup black beans

¾ cup shredded sharp cheddar

4 poached eggs *(see page 89)*

½ cup Smoked Tomato Butter Sauce, or more to taste *(see page 73)*

½ cup sour cream

Chive Oil *(see page 190)*

Smoked Paprika Oil *(see page 191)*

1 tablespoon chives, finely minced

jalapeño slices, for garnish

1 ripe avocado, sliced

1. In frying pan, add a teaspoon or so of olive oil and cook the tortillas until lightly brown on each side, about 2 minutes total, adding more oil as needed. Set on paper towel until ready to serve.

2. In same frying pan used for the tortillas, add a tablespoon of olive oil and add the sausage, onions, and poblano peppers and cook over medium heat until sausage is cooked and vegetables are lightly browned, about 15 minutes.

3. Fold in black beans and cook another 3 minutes. Lower to simmer and cover until ready to plate.

To serve:

Place a fried tortilla on each plate. Divide the sausage and vegetable mixture among the plates. Top with shredded cheddar, a poached egg, a couple tablespoons of the smoked tomato sauce, butter and a dollop of sour cream. Drizzle the chive and smoked paprika oils. Garnish with minced chives, jalapeno slices, and 2 slices of avocado.

CHEESE BLINTZ CUSTARD,
page **126**

CHAPTER 5

Sweet Dishes and Bites

Many of these dishes make a nice first course, a light dessert, or a lovely addition to a brunch buffet. They offer a nice balance between sweet and tart from fresh fruit.

White Peaches, Honey Cardamom Mascarpone, *and* Raspberry–Filled Crepes *with* Raspberry Coulis

Serves 4

8 ounces mascarpone, room temperature

2 tablespoons honey

¼ teaspoon cardamom

¼ teaspoon ground coriander

1 teaspoon orange zest

4 Basic Crepes *(see recipe below)*

1 ripe white peach, cored and thinly sliced

1 cup of fresh raspberries

powdered sugar, for dusting

Raspberry Coulis *(see page 186)*

mint sprig, for garnish

1. Mix mascarpone, honey, cardamom, coriander, and orange zest and let sit to meld, about an hour or so.

2. Spread about 1½ tablespoons of the mascarpone mixture on the center of each crepe. Top with 2–3 thin peach slices and a few raspberries. Fold into an envelope and place seam side down. Dust with powdered sugar and drizzle with Raspberry Coulis. Garnish with a mint sprig and a peach slice.

Basic Sweet Crepes

Makes 12 crepes

1⅓ cups milk (I use 2%)

4 large eggs

1⅓ cups flour

1 teaspoon vanilla

2 tablespoons sugar

pinch of salt

½ stick butter, melted

To make the crepes:

1. Mix the milk, eggs, flour, vanilla, sugar, and salt in a blender, scraping down the sides to incorporate all the ingredients. Pour the melted butter through the opening in the lid and mix for another few seconds. Let the batter sit in the refrigerator at least 30 minutes or up to one day.

2. Remove the batter from refrigerator and let sit at room temperature for 30–60 minutes. Heat a shallow nonstick frying pan or steel crepe pan, 8–9 inches in diameter, over medium-high heat. Coat with nonstick cooking spray or butter. Add a small amount of batter and swirl it around to coat the pan in a thin layer. Heat until the edges just turn brown, about 1½–2 minutes, and flip to cook for another 30 seconds or so. Remove to a piece of wax paper and repeat with remaining batter, stacking the crepes.

White Peaches *and* Cinnamon Ricotta–Filled Crepes Topped *with* Cinnamon Sugar

Serves 4

8 ounces ricotta

2 tablespoons brown sugar

2 teaspoons cinnamon, divided

4 Basic Crepes *(see recipe above)*

1 ripe white peach, sliced

mint sprig, for garnish

cinnamon sugar, for dusting

1. In a blender or food processor, mix ricotta, brown sugar, and 1 teaspoon cinnamon until smooth (a smooth ricotta makes a big difference).

2. Divide the ricotta mixture among the crepes and top with 2–3 peach slices. Fold into an envelope and place seam side down.

3. Mix 1 tablespoon granulated sugar with 1 teaspoon cinnamon and put into a shaker. Dust crepes with cinnamon sugar and garnish with peach slices and a mint sprig.

Banana, Mascarpone, *and* Toasted Almond–Filled Crepes *with* Chocolate Ganache

Serves 4

8 ounces mascarpone, room temperature

2 tablespoons honey

1 tablespoon almond liqueur

2 tablespoons raw almonds

4 **Basic Crepes** *(see page 116)*

1 ripe large banana, sliced about ¼ inch thick or less

powdered sugar, for dusting

Chocolate Ganache *(see page 186)*

mint sprig, for garnish

1. Mix mascarpone, honey, and almond liqueur and let sit to meld, about an hour or so.

2. Toast almonds on a sheet pan at 300 degrees for about 10–12 minutes, until fragrant and slightly golden. Let cool.

3. Spread about 1½ tablespoons of the mascarpone mixture on the center of each crepe. Top with 2–3 banana slices and a few toasted almonds. Fold into an envelope and place seam side down. Dust with powdered sugar and drizzle with chocolate ganache. Garnish with a banana slice, toasted almonds, and a mint sprig.

Chocolate, Banana, *and* Raspberry French Toast

This was one of our signature sweet entrées at the inn. We'd alternate daily between sweet and savory, but this was often requested when the guests made their reservations. It's really a simple dish dressed with a couple of simple sauces that create a symphony when combined.

Serves 4

4 large eggs

1 cup half and half

½ cup granulated sugar

¼ teaspoon salt

½ teaspoon vanilla extract

3 ounces cream cheese, softened

8 slices thick-cut brioche bread/challah

2 small ripe bananas

powdered sugar, for dusting

Raspberry Coulis *(see page 186)*

Chocolate Ganache *(see page 186)*

fresh raspberries, for garnish

1. Preheat the oven to 325 degrees.

2. Combine the eggs, half and half, sugar, salt, and vanilla in blender and mix for about 5 seconds. Pour into a wide bowl for dipping.

3. Spread the softened cream cheese thinly on all eight slices of bread.

4. Thinly slice the bananas and divide among four slices of bread, layering evenly.

5. Place the top slice of bread on top of the layer of bananas, with the cream cheese side facing down. Dip each sandwich into the egg mixture to coat, making sure to soak thoroughly.

6. Fry on griddle or skillet over medium heat until browned on both sides, about 4–5 minutes per side.

7. Place on a parchment-lined sheet, cover with foil, and bake until the center is heated through, about 10–15 minutes. Remove the foil and cook another 3 minutes to dry the surface of the bread.

8. Remove from the oven and let sit for 2 minutes before slicing on a diagonal. Dust with powdered sugar and serve with a drizzle of raspberry coulis and chocolate ganache, accompanied by fresh raspberries and sliced bananas.

Chocolate *and* Banana Bread Pudding *with* Mascarpone, Ricotta, *and* Chocolate Chips

If you are a fan of classic Italian cannoli, this is for you. I've combined a few of my favorites into one dish. Creamy ricotta and rich chocolate! Top this off with a scoop of vanilla ice cream and you have a decadent dessert!

Serves 6 to 8

1-pound loaf of challah or brioche

7 eggs

2 cups half and half

1 cup heavy cream

¾ cup sugar

1 teaspoon vanilla extract

¼ teaspoon salt

8 ounces mascarpone, room temperature

4 ounces creamy ricotta

1 egg yolk

2 tablespoons honey

1 cup chocolate chips or chopped bittersweet chocolate

2 ripe bananas, sliced about ¼ inch thick

4 tablespoons butter, melted

3 tablespoons sugar, for dusting

1. Cube the bread and let sit out to dry for a couple of hours.

2. Combine the eggs, half and half, heavy cream, sugar, vanilla, and salt in a blender and mix for about 4–5 seconds.

3. Mix the mascarpone, ricotta, egg yolk, and honey until smooth (in a blender is best). Fold in chocolate chips. Set aside.

4. Put half of the bread into a 9x13-inch rectangular or oval baking dish. Add about half of the sliced bananas. Dollop the mascarpone mixture on top of the bread and bananas, then top with remaining bread cubes and remaining bananas. Pour the egg custard mixture into the pan and let sit for at least 6–8 hours or as long as overnight. If refrigerated, let sit at room temperature about 45 minutes before baking.

5. Pour melted butter on top of the bread pudding and dust with 3 tablespoons of sugar. Bake at 350 degrees, covered, for 35 minutes. Uncover and continue to bake for 15 minutes to lightly brown the top.

6. Let sit for 10-15 minutes before serving.

Monte Cristo *with* Ham, Maple Mustard, Pears, Havarti, *and* Raspberry Coulis

This dish was inspired by a famous French-style crepe restaurant near my hometown of Bethesda, Maryland, that served a wonderful fried Monte Cristo. This is my griddled version for breakfast. It satisfies guests with a sweet or savory preference—and it became one of the favorites.

Serves 4

4 large eggs

1 cup half and half

¼ cup sweet brown mustard

½ cup plus 2 tablespoons maple syrup

¼ teaspoon salt

8 slices of challah or other thick-cut egg bread or brioche

6 slices of thinly sliced smoked ham

8 slices of Havarti or Monterey Jack

1 ripe but firm Bosc pear, sliced

fresh raspberries, for garnish

Raspberry Coulis *(see page 186)*

raspberry preserves (optional)

1. Preheat the oven to 325 degrees.

2. Mix the eggs, half and half, mustard, 2 tablespoons of the maple syrup, and salt in a blender for 5 seconds. Pour into a wide bowl for dipping.

3. Layer four slices of the bread with the ham, cheese, sliced pear, and another layer of cheese, then top with the remaining 4 slices of bread. Cut in half. Dip the sandwich halves into the egg mixture and fry on a griddle over medium heat until brown on both sides, about 5 minutes. Move the sandwiches to a parchment-lined cookie sheet when done. Cover with foil and bake in the oven for 15 minutes, then uncover and bake for 5 more minutes, until completely heated through.

4. Serve the two halves on a plate with fresh raspberries, maple syrup, and raspberry coulis (alternatively you could serve it with a small ramekin of raspberry preserves instead). Sometimes I add diced kiwi for color and a light acidic bite.

Dana's Tip

In my most recent version I use a homemade raspberry maple mustard instead of maple syrup and preserves. This combines both flavors in one sauce. I buy Hannaford Inspirations brand Maine Maple Mustard, which is absolutely delicious and key to the flavor of this dish, if you can find it, but if not, use a sweet brown mustard and add ½ cup maple syrup instead.

Raspberry Maple Mustard

½ cup **Raspberry Coulis** *(see page 186)*

½ cup **Hannaford Inspirations brand Maine Maple Mustard**

¼ cup **maple syrup**

¼ cup **heavy cream**

Blend all ingredients and keep in squeeze bottle in refrigerator for up to 5 days.

Cheese Blintz Custard *with* Blackberry, Raspberry, *and* Mango Coulis

This dish combines the flavor and ingredients of a cheese-filled blintz or crepe, but in a baked custard, cake-like form. It is a dish inspired by one of my favorite brunch recipes, made with store-bought blintzes, that my mother and cousin would make at brunch for family gatherings or holidays. I decided to use our local Maine blackberries because they seem sweeter and less tart than the mass-produced variety. And why not keep it local when I could? Add blackberry, raspberry, and mango coulis and you have delicious art on a plate. Guests would come into the kitchen while I was "painting" with my sauces and get such a kick out of me because sometimes I'd do every plate with a different design. This was one of the most photographed dishes!

Serves 8

Filling

¹/₃ cup granulated sugar

1 egg yolk

1½ cups cottage cheese (I use 4%, but you can also use 1%)

8 ounces softened cream cheese

1 tablespoon vanilla extract

In a food processor, mix the sugar, egg yolk, cottage cheese, cream cheese, and vanilla and set aside.

Batter

1½ sticks unsalted butter, softened

1¼ cups sour cream, room temperature

¾ cup granulated sugar

5 eggs, room temperature

1¾ cups plus 1 tablespoon flour

5 teaspoons baking powder

2 tablespoons milk (2% or whole)

½ cup orange juice (low or no pulp)

To make the batter, in a stand mixer, add the butter, sour cream, and sugar and combine until smooth. Add the eggs one at a time while mixing and blend again until smooth. Add the flour and baking powder and mix on low while adding the milk and orange juice. Blend until just mixed, though the batter may remain slightly lumpy.

Garnish

Mango Coulis *(see page 187)*

Blackberry Coulis *(see page 187)*

Raspberry Coulis *(see page 186)*

fresh blackberries

powdered sugar

1. Preheat the oven to 325 degrees.

2. Liberally coat a 9×13 glass baking dish with butter or vegetable oil. (Glass enables you to see how much the bottom begins to brown so you can move it to a higher rack and/or lower the oven if needed.) Layer half of the batter on the bottom. Carefully dollop the filling over the batter, keeping it at least a half-inch from the edges. Top the filling with the remaining batter.

3. Bake, uncovered, for 45 minutes, until lightly browned. Cover and lower the heat to 275 degrees for another 10 minutes. Remove from oven and allow to rest for 10 minutes, covered, before cutting. This allows the filling to set and not fall apart when slicing. (I learned this the hard way!)

4. Serve with mango coulis, blackberry coulis, raspberry coulis, and fresh blackberries and dust with powdered sugar.

Dana's Tip

The batter and filling for this can be made a day ahead and stored in the refrigerator. Make sure you use double-acting baking powder and let it sit at room temperature for about 30–60 minutes before assembling and placing in the oven to bake.

Blueberry Oatmeal Streusel French Toast *with* Warm Rum Sauce

There are thousands of baked French toast recipes out there; with this one I've created bread pudding meets baked French toast meets egg custard. The crunchy pecan streusel topping is addictive—but then so is the rum sauce. I used to walk into the dining room at the inn with my squeeze bottle to offer more. Seriously! Fresh sliced peaches make a nice accompaniment to this dish.

Serves 8 to 10

1-pound loaf of challah or egg bread/brioche

1 pint fresh blueberries

8 large eggs

3 cups half and half

¼ cup light brown sugar

1 tablespoon vanilla extract

1 tablespoon ground cinnamon

1 stick unsalted butter, softened

1 cup packed light brown sugar

2 tablespoons dark corn syrup

1 cup chopped pecans

1 cup thick rolled oats (not instant or quick cooking)

¼ teaspoon ground nutmeg (fresh grated is best)

Maple Rum Sauce *(see page 185)*

fresh peaches, sliced, for garnish

fresh blueberries, for garnish

1. Preheat the oven to 350 degrees. Coat a 9x13 baking dish with butter or vegetable oil.

2. Cut the bread into 1-inch cubes and layer half evenly in baking dish. Sprinkle blueberries on top. Layer remaining bread.

3. Combine the eggs, half and half, sugar, vanilla, and cinnamon in a blender for about 5 seconds. (If mixing in a stand mixer, beat for 2 minutes on medium-high.) Pour the mixture over bread.

Dana's Tip

In addition to being an easy make-ahead dish, this freezes and rewarms beautifully if you send your friends and family home with leftovers.

4. For the topping, combine the butter, brown sugar, and corn syrup in a mixing bowl outfitted with a paddle and mix on medium-high until creamy, about 2 minutes. Fold in the pecans, oats, and nutmeg and mix just to combine.

5. Dollop and carefully spread the topping onto the top of the bread. Cover with foil and refrigerate overnight.

6. Bring the dish to room temperature, or at least 45 minutes, before baking. When ready to bake, preheat the oven to 375 degrees.

7. Place the dish over a rimmed baking sheet, as it will drip when baking. (Oven fires are not a good thing—please, as my mother says, "Do as I say, not as I do!")

8. Bake covered in foil for about 40 minutes. Remove the foil and bake for another 10 minutes. Reduce the oven to 275 degrees and let sit in the oven for another 10 minutes.

9. Remove from the oven and let rest for 15 minutes before slicing—it is very important to let it rest before slicing or it will not hold its shape and will fall apart when plating. Slice down the middle of the pan, then into 4 or 5 slices across.

10. Drizzle the warm maple rum sauce over the top of each slice and serve with fresh sliced peaches and blueberries.

Classic Malted Belgian Waffles *with* Grand Marnier Maple Syrup *and* Toasted Coconut *and* Macadamias

The inspiration for this dish came from a family vacation in Hawaii when I was sixteen. Breakfast each morning at our hotel included waffles and pancakes to order, but the best part was the selection of toppings, which included coconut syrup and macadamia nuts. This is my twist on that memorable breakfast.

Makes 12 4-inch Belgian-style waffles

2¼ cups flour

4 tablespoons granulated sugar

⅛ teaspoon salt

½ cup canola or vegetable oil

1½ cups 2% milk

1 egg

¼ cup malted milk powder

2 tablespoons baking powder

shredded coconut

chopped macadamias

1½ cups maple syrup

2 tablespoons Grand Marnier

juice from 1 orange

zest of 1 orange, for garnish

Fresh Whipped Cream *(page 205)*

Dana's Tip

To make pancakes using this recipe, just add 1 more egg and ¼ cup less milk. Classic Maine blueberry pancakes! Or for ginger spice pancakes, add ¼ teaspoon nutmeg, ¼ teaspoon ginger (fresh if available), and ½ teaspoon cinnamon. The spice version is especially delicious in cooler months

131

1. In a large bowl, combine the flour, sugar, salt, oil, milk, egg, malted milk powder, and baking powder and mix with a whisk until well combined.

2. Heat a waffle iron and coat with cooking spray. Ladle the batter into the iron and cook until steam starts to diminish and the waffle appears golden brown and crispy, about 8 minutes, or longer to your liking (I often cook them longer than the manufacturer recommends for a crispier waffle).

3. While waffles are cooking, spread the coconut and macadamia nuts on a sheet pan lined with parchment and toast in oven at 300 degrees until very lightly browned.

4. In a small pot, combine the maple syrup, Grand Marnier, and orange juice, and stir until heated through.

5. Serve with orange maple syrup and garnish with toasted coconut and macadamia nuts, orange zest, and whipped cream.

Dark Chocolate Waffles *with* Fresh Raspberries, Raspberry Coulis, Chocolate Ganache, *and* Vanilla Frozen Yogurt

With yogurt, it's breakfast, right? These are a bit of brownie meets waffle. Any way you look at it, they're delicious and indulgent!

Makes 6 round, thick Belgian waffles

2 cups all-purpose flour

½ cup high-quality Dutch-processed dark cocoa powder

2 teaspoons baking powder

1 teaspoon baking soda

¼ teaspoon sea salt

3 large eggs, separated

½ cup lightly packed brown sugar

½ cup granulated sugar

2¼ cups buttermilk

¼ cup vegetable oil

1 tablespoon vanilla extract

4 tablespoons unsalted butter, melted

1 cup bittersweet chocolate, finely chopped (or chocolate chips)

mint sprig, for garnish

Raspberry Coulis *(see page 186)*

fresh raspberries, for garnish

Chocolate Ganache *(see page 186)*

vanilla frozen yogurt

1. Whisk together the flour, cocoa powder, baking powder, baking soda, and salt in a large bowl. Whisk together the egg yolks and sugars until smooth. Add the buttermilk, oil, and vanilla and whisk until combined. Add the wet mixture to the dry mixture and mix until just combined. Fold in the butter and chocolate. Whip the egg whites in a medium bowl until soft peaks form, then fold the whites into the batter.

2. Heat a waffle iron and coat with cooking spray. Ladle the batter into the iron and cook until steam starts to diminish and the waffle appears golden brown and crispy, about 5-6 minutes, or longer to your liking. (I often cook them longer than the manufacturer recommends for a crispier waffle but since these are dark chocolate, it's harder to gauge when they are overdone and burnt chocolate isn't tasty!) Repeat with the remaining batter. Serve with raspberry coulis, fresh raspberries, a drizzle of chocolate ganache, and a scoop of vanilla frozen yogurt.

Baked Oatmeal Cake *with* Fresh Strawberries, Rhubarb Sauce, *and* Warm Vanilla Cream

This was one of the most surprising and most often requested recipes we served at the inn, probably because of its simplicity and the health benefits of oats. It was surprising because many people who don't typically like oatmeal (myself included) really enjoyed this because of its cake-like texture. I even kept preprinted cards with the inn's logo and the recipe at the checkout desk in anticipation of the request! Give it a try: You just might convert some oatmeal naysayers, like I did.

Serves 8 to 12

½ cup vegetable oil

½ cup walnut oil (if you don't have walnut, just use 1 full cup of vegetable oil)

1 stick butter, melted

1½ cups granulated sugar

5 large eggs

1 tablespoon ground cinnamon

2 teaspoons baking powder

1 teaspoon vanilla extract

1½ teaspoons salt

2¾ cups half and half

6 cups thick-cut rolled oats (not quick cook or instant)

Warm Vanilla Cream *(see recipe below)*

Rhubarb Sauce *(see page 185)*

sliced strawberries

1. Combine the oils, butter, sugar, eggs, cinnamon, baking powder, vanilla, salt, and half and half in a mixer and beat with whisk attachment until well combined. (You can also use a blender, which is my favorite way to blend any egg/dairy mixture, and then pour into a bowl before adding the oats.) Add the oats to the bowl and mix thoroughly.

2. Pour the mixture into a well-greased 9x13 glass baking dish, cover with plastic wrap, and chill in the refrigerator overnight. Letting it sit overnight is an important step.

3. Remove the dish from refrigerator and allow to sit at room temperature at least 30 minutes. Preheat the oven to 350 degrees.

4. Bake, uncovered, for 30–35 minutes, until lightly brown on top. Cut into squares, place in a shallow bowl, and top with warm vanilla cream and rhubarb sauce and garnish with some fresh sliced strawberries. This freezes and rewarms beautifully. So does the delicious rhubarb sauce!

Warm Vanilla Cream

1 cup whole milk
1 teaspoon vanilla
1 tablespoon powdered sugar

To make warm vanilla cream:

Mix together the milk, vanilla, and sugar and warm in saucepan or microwave. Serve warm.

Blueberry, Mascarpone, *and* Lemon Zest Bread Pudding

This dish is a transformation of the blueberry lemon French toast recipe in the first edition. I wanted a creamier version than just a baked French toast dish, but more than just griddled French toast. I thought I might just serve the original recipe with a dollop of the lemon zest ricotta, but then I combined the two. When you get a bite of the creamy lemon zest ricotta, you look forward to that next bite!

Serves 6 to 8

1-pound loaf of challah or brioche

7 eggs

2 cups half and half

1 cup heavy cream

¾ cup sugar, plus 2 tablespoons

¼ teaspoon salt

juice from 1 lemon

8 ounces mascarpone, room temperature

4 ounces creamy ricotta

1 egg yolk

2 tablespoons honey

zest from 1 lemon

1 pint fresh blueberries

4 tablespoons butter

1. Cube the bread and let sit out to dry for a couple of hours.

2. Combine eggs, half and half, heavy cream, ¾ cup sugar, salt, and lemon juice in a blender and mix for about 4–5 seconds.

3. Using either a food processor (my preference for a really smooth mixture) or a stand mixer with the paddle attachment, mix mascarpone, ricotta, egg yolk, honey, and lemon zest until smooth. Set aside.

4. Put half of the bread into a 9×13 rectangular or oval baking dish. Add about half of the blueberries. Dollop the mascarpone mixture on top of the bread and blueberries, then top with the remaining bread cubes and blueberries. Pour the egg custard mixture into the pan and let sit at least 6–8 hours or as long as overnight. If refrigerated, let sit at room temperature about 45 minutes before baking.

5. Melt butter and pour on top of the bread pudding and dust with 2 tablespoons of sugar. Bake at 350 degrees, covered, for 35 minutes. Uncover and continue to bake for 15 minutes to lightly brown the top.

6. Let sit for 10 minutes before serving.

Date and Bacon Tartlets
with Goat Cheese *and* Honey

This is a well-balanced bite, satisfying both the sweet tooth and savory preference. These cute tartlets make a great addition to a cheese board.

Makes 12 to 16 tartlets, depending on the size of your muffin tin

1 cup goat cheese, room temperature

2 tablespoons honey

½ teaspoon kosher salt

½ teaspoon black pepper

6 strips thick-cut bacon

¾ cup chopped medjool dates

1 package of pie crust dough

1. Mix goat cheese, honey, salt, and pepper until well combined.

2. Dice and sauté bacon over medium heat until just shy of crisp. Drain on paper towel and cool.

3. Mix chopped dates with bacon.

4. Roll out pie dough and cut each crust into 6–8 discs, depending on the size of your cookie or biscuit cutter. Coat a muffin tin with nonstick cooking spray or butter. Place a disc of dough in the bottom of each muffin tin cavity, pressing down and making sure the sides are pressed against the tin. Bake for about 8–10 minutes until lightly browned. Let cool. Remove tart shells to a plate.

5. Fill each tart with a tablespoon of the goat cheese mixture. Top with a tablespoon or so of the bacon and date mixture. Serve at room temperature.

Lemon Basil Panna Cotta Topped
with Fresh Strawberries *and* Mango

If you haven't tried basil with fresh fruit, you should! The combination here is subtle and refreshing. [I used mini Bundt tins so that when they were turned out onto a plate the panna cottas had a nice, finished look. You could also use individual ramekins.]

Serves 8

1 envelope unflavored gelatin

2 tablespoons cold water

1¼ cups heavy cream

¾ cup half and half

¼ cup Basil Simple Syrup *(page 182)*

¼ cup granulated sugar

4 ounces cream cheese, room temperature

zest from 1 lemon

juice from ½ lemon

6 large basil leaves, finely chopped

1 ripe mango, diced

8 strawberries, thinly sliced

basil sprigs

vegetable oil, for coating muffin tin or ramekins

1. Mix the gelatin and water in a small saucepan and let soften for 2 minutes. Heat over low until the gelatin is dissolved, about 1 minute. Remove from heat.

2. In a medium saucepan, add the cream, half and half, simple syrup, and sugar and bring to a boil over medium-high heat. Once just boiling, remove the pan from the heat and add the cream cheese, lemon zest, lemon juice, basil, and melted gelatin mixture. Mix well. Cool to room temperature.

3. Coat a ½-cup muffin tin (or any standard-size muffin tin or individual 6-ounce ramekins) with vegetable oil and fill eight of them evenly with the cream. Cover with plastic wrap and chill overnight, or at least 6 hours.

4. Run a sharp knife around the edge to loosen the suction. Carefully pop out onto plates. Garnish with diced mango, sliced strawberries, and a basil sprig.

Caramelized Rosemary, Honey, and Black Pepper Panna Cotta *with* Sugar Toasted Pistachios

This is one of my favorite variations of panna cotta. The complex, rich rosemary honey and black pepper are subtle enough to not overpower the overall flavor. The result is a nicely balanced dessert.

Serves 8

½ cup shelled pistachios

1 tablespoon sugar

1 envelope unflavored gelatin

2 tablespoons cold water

½ cup honey

1-inch lemon peel

1 sprig of rosemary, bruised

1 teaspoon cracked black pepper

1½ cups heavy cream

¾ cup half and half

¼ cup granulated sugar

4 ounces cream cheese, room temperature

rosemary sprigs, for garnish

1. Preheat the oven to 300 degrees. Lay pistachios on a sheet pan, sprinkle with sugar and toast for 15 minutes until fragrant and lightly toasted, tossing about midway through for a more subtle flavor.

2. Mix the gelatin and water in a small saucepan and let soften for 2 minutes. Heat over low until the gelatin is dissolved, about 1 minute. Remove from heat.

3. In another small saucepan, heat honey, lemon peel, and rosemary (muddle it in the pan) over medium heat for about 6–8 minutes, until the rosemary is fully infused and honey has slightly darkened. Add pepper. Let cool at least 15 minutes or so. Discard rosemary.

4. In a medium saucepan, add the cream, half and half, and sugar and bring to a boil over medium-high heat. Once just boiling, remove the pan from the heat and add ¼ cup of the honey, the cream cheese, and the melted gelatin mixture. Mix well. Cool to room temperature.

5. Coat a ½-cup muffin tin (or any standard-size muffin tin or individual 6-ounce ramekins) with vegetable oil and fill eight of them evenly with the cream. Cover with plastic wrap and chill overnight, or at least 6 hours.

6. Run a sharp knife around the edge to loosen the suction. Carefully pop out onto plates and garnish with a drizzle of the remaining honey, a few toasted sugar pistachios, and a rosemary sprig.

Vanilla Bean Panna Cotta *with* Fresh Berries *and* Raspberry Coulis

This is a basic recipe that can be flavored a variety of ways. My twist is the addition of cream cheese. I used to serve this vanilla-flavored version with raspberry coulis, fresh raspberries, and blueberries on the Fourth of July at the inn.

Serves 8

1 envelope unflavored gelatin

2 tablespoons cold water

1½ cups heavy cream

¾ cup half and half

⅓ cup plus 1 tablespoon granulated sugar

4 ounces cream cheese, room temperature

1 vanilla bean (or 1 teaspoon vanilla extract)

Raspberry Coulis *(see page 186)*

fresh raspberries, for garnish

fresh blueberries, for garnish

> **Dana's Tip**
> *Try flavoring the cream with different extracts and zests. You're limited only by your imagination. At the inn we served coconut-flavored panna cotta with lime zest and garnished it with kiwi and watermelon slices. But I've included a similar recipe for a coconut cream sauce for kiwi and watermelon in this cookbook (see page 000). In cooler months I like to serve the caramelized rosemary honey black pepper panna cotta since it's a bit richer (see page 000).*

1. Mix the gelatin and water in a small saucepan and let soften for 2 minutes. Heat over low until the gelatin is dissolved, about 1 minute. Remove from heat.

2. In a medium saucepan, add the cream, half and half, and sugar and bring to a boil over medium-high heat. Once just boiling, remove the pan from the heat and add the cream cheese, vanilla, and melted gelatin mixture. Split and scrape the seeds from the vanilla bean and add to the mixture. Mix well. Cool to room temperature.

3. Coat a ½-cup muffin tin (or any standard-size muffin tin or individual 6-ounce ramekins) with vegetable oil and fill eight of them evenly with the cream. Cover with plastic wrap and chill overnight, or at least 4–6 hours.

4. Run a sharp knife around the edge to loosen the suction. Carefully pop out onto plates drizzled with raspberry coulis and garnish with fresh raspberries and blueberries.

TRIPLE CHOCOLATE-CHIP
MALTED COOKIES, *page 147*

CHAPTER 6

Baked Goods

White Chocolate Chip Macadamia Coconut Cookies

I used to make these with macadamia nuts at the inn, and they were always a favorite. Any nuts can be used. There was a very special elderly couple who stayed at our inn several times. They referred to these cookies as "theirs," so I'd send a batch to them at holiday time. It's amazing what the memory of a simple little cookie can do for the soul—and for the person giving them.

Makes about 36 cookies

1⅔ cups flour

¾ teaspoon baking powder

½ teaspoon baking soda

½ teaspoon salt

¾ cup light brown sugar

⅓ cup granulated sugar

1 tablespoon vanilla extract

1½ sticks unsalted butter, softened

1 large egg

1½ cups white chocolate chips

1 cup shredded coconut

¾ cup chopped macadamias

1. Preheat the oven to 325 degrees.

2. Combine the flour, baking powder, baking soda, and salt and set aside.

3. In a mixing bowl, combine the sugars, vanilla, and butter and mix on medium speed until blended. Add the egg and continue mixing until smooth. Add the flour mixture and blend on low speed for about 10 seconds. Fold in the white chocolate chips, coconut, and nuts.

4. Using a 1½- to 2-inch cookie scoop (or heaping tablespoon), scoop out onto a parchment- or silicone-lined baking sheet.

5. Bake 10–12 minutes, until just lightly browned. For chewy cookies, bake 9–10 minutes; for crispy cookies, bake 12–13 minutes.

Triple Chocolate-Chip Malted Cookies

I call these Chocolate Dreams! Adding Nutella and malt powder keeps them moist and chewy—triple chocolatey, actually. They're crisp on the outside and chewy on the inside, and I think that's the best way to enjoy them.

Makes about 42 cookies

2¼ cups flour

¾ teaspoon baking powder

½ teaspoon baking soda

¼ teaspoon salt

¾ cup dark brown sugar

⅓ cup granulated sugar

¼ cup sweetened condensed milk

½ cup malted milk powder

1 cup cocoa powder

1 tablespoon vanilla extract

1 cup Nutella

2 sticks unsalted butter, softened

2 large eggs

1½ cups semisweet chocolate chips

1. Preheat the oven to 350 degrees.

2. Combine the flour, baking powder, baking soda, and salt and set aside.

3. In mixing bowl, combine the sugars, condensed milk, malt powder, cocoa powder, vanilla, Nutella, and butter and mix on medium speed until blended. Add the eggs and mix until smooth. Add the flour mixture and mix on low for 6–8 seconds. Fold in the chocolate chips.

4. Using a 1½- to 2-inch cookie scoop (or heaping tablespoon), scoop out onto a parchment- or silicone-lined baking sheet.

5. Bake for 10–12 minutes, until just lightly browned. These cookies will set up once cool, but you'll want to pull them out of the oven before they're firm to the touch.

Dana's Tip

For regular chocolate-chip cookies, just eliminate the Nutella and cocoa powder. But don't leave out the malt powder—that's what gives it that something extra!

Chocolate Rum Balls

Our signature at the Kingsleigh—we put these in all guest rooms on a daily basis. These are reminiscent of fudge, truffle, and brownie all combined into one. They also hold up in warmer months because they're a cookie base, which makes them less messy for summer picnics. I used to have my wonderful housekeepers help me roll triple batches just to keep up with the demand!

Makes about 30

8 ounces bittersweet or semisweet chocolate

½ cup dark or spiced rum

3 tablespoons corn syrup

2½ cups finely ground Oreo or chocolate wafer cookies

½ cup granulated sugar

1. Melt the chocolate with the rum and corn syrup in small saucepan over low heat.

2. Remove from the heat and add the ground cookie crumbs, mixing thoroughly to combine. Allow the mixture to set up at room temperature for a few hours or in the refrigerator for about an hour.

3. Roll into 1½-inch balls, then dip into a bowl with the granulated sugar to coat. Set on a sheet pan or flat plate to chill in the refrigerator until ready to serve. Keep in an airtight container in the refrigerator for 2 weeks or in the freezer for 2 months.

Chocolate Cherry Tart

This is wonderful as an afternoon treat with coffee or tea. Add a scoop of vanilla bean ice cream and you have a perfect dessert.

Serves 8

4 cups fresh sweet Bing cherries, pitted

½ cup sugar

¼ cup port wine plus 2 tablespoons

1 tablespoon chocolate balsamic vinegar (I use Fiore);
  if not available, use an aged balsamic

1 teaspoon arrowroot powder, dissolved in a couple tablespoons
  of the port wine

2 teaspoons cocoa powder

1 sheet frozen puff pastry, thawed

4 ounces softened cream cheese

4 ounces shaved chocolate (or chocolate chips)

1. Preheat the oven to 375 degrees.

2. Mix the pitted cherries with the sugar, port, balsamic vinegar, dissolved arrowroot powder, and cocoa and put into medium saucepan. Cook over medium heat until the sauce comes to a boil. Remove cherries and boil sauce 2–3 minutes longer to thicken. Remove from heat, return cherries to the sauce, and allow to rest. (If you can't find cherries and use frozen, make sure they are completely drained before you begin.)

3. Press the puff pastry sheet into a 9-inch shallow, greased baking dish or tart pan.

4. Spread the softened cream cheese on the pastry. Spread the chocolate shavings (or chips) evenly over the cream cheese. Then, using a slotted spoon so that you leave some of the sauce out, place the cherries in a single layer over chocolate.

5. Bake for 35 minutes. Allow to cool at least 20 minutes before serving.

Dana's Gourmet Granola

We used to package and sell this to the local market in Southwest Harbor but were unable to keep up with the demand while the inn was open during the peak season. We offered this to our guests every morning with fruit and yogurt before the plated fruit course and entrée.

Makes approximately 5 cups

½ cup vegetable oil

¼ cup honey

1 teaspoon cinnamon

1 teaspoon vanilla extract

¼ cup brown sugar

2 cups thick-cut oats
  (not quick cooking)

¾ cup shredded coconut

¾ cup sliced almonds

½ cup pecans

½ cup pumpkin seeds

½ cup dried cranberries

½ cup golden raisins

1. Preheat the oven to 325 degrees. Line a rimmed baking sheet with parchment paper.

2. Combine the oil and honey in a small glass mixing cup and microwave for 90 seconds. Add the cinnamon and vanilla and set aside.

3. In a large mixing bowl, combine the brown sugar, oats, coconut, almonds, pecans, pumpkin seeds, cranberries, and raisins and mix well. Add the oil and honey mixture and mix with spatula until very well coated.

4. Spread the granola onto a baking sheet and bake until just lightly browned, about 25–30 minutes, stirring halfway through to ensure even cooking.

5. Store in an airtight container in the pantry for up to 1 week. The cooked granola freezes very well and keeps for a couple months, especially when using a vacuum sealer.

Pecan Shortbread

These are an adaptation of my mother-in-law's Pecan Puffs, my husband's favorite cookie. They're wonderful with a cup of tea or coffee in the afternoon, though they're not bad at breakfast, either.

Makes about 18 bars

2 sticks unsalted butter, softened

⅓ cup granulated sugar

2 teaspoons vanilla extract

2 cups finely ground pecans

2 cups flour

powdered sugar, for garnish

halved pecans, for garnish

1. Preheat the oven to 300 degrees.

2. Using a stand or hand mixer, cream together the butter and sugar until smooth. Add the vanilla, pecans, and flour and stir gently until fully combined.

3. Press the mixture into a glass or light colored (to prevent browning too much) baking dish coated with butter.

4. Bake for about 25–30 minutes, until just lightly browned. Remove from the oven, let cool 2–3 minutes, then cut into squares while warm and then let fully cool in the pan.

5. Once cool, sprinkle the powdered sugar on top and garnish with a pecan half.

Cream Scones

Cream scones are a cross between a classic scone and a light cake. The addition of heavy cream makes them not quite as crumbly as traditional scones. This maple version is my favorite, at breakfast or in the afternoon with coffee or tea.

Makes 6 to 8 scones

¼ cup plus 2 tablespoons granulated sugar

1 stick unsalted butter, softened

½ cup plus 1 tablespoon heavy cream

2 eggs

2 cups flour

¼ teaspoon salt

2 teaspoons baking powder

1 teaspoon vanilla extract

1 tablespoon heavy cream

2 tablespoons raw sugar

1. Preheat the oven to 350 degrees.

2. Using a stand or hand mixer, cream together the sugar and butter until combined. Add ½ cup of the cream and one egg and continue to mix until smooth. Add the flour, salt, baking powder, and vanilla and mix until just incorporated.

3. Roll the mixture out on a floured surface into a circle about ½–¾ inch thick. Cut into 6–8 wedges. Place the wedges on a parchment- or silicone-lined baking sheet. In a small bowl, mix together the remaining egg and tablespoon of heavy cream. Brush the mixture on top of the wedges and then sprinkle with the raw sugar. Bake for 15 minutes, until lightly browned.

Maple Glaze

½ stick of unsalted butter

pinch of salt

1½ cups powdered sugar

1 teaspoon maple extract

1 tablespoon maple syrup

3 tablespoons whole milk

To make the maple glaze:

1. In a small saucepan, add the butter and cook over medium-low heat until browned. Watch carefully so the butter doesn't burn! When browned, strain through a sieve and add a pinch of salt to taste.

2. In a medium bowl, whisk the browned butter together with the powdered sugar, maple extract, maple syrup, and 2 tablespoons milk. Whisk together and add more milk as necessary until the desired consistency is reached. Pour over the scones and let cool before serving.

Dana's Tip

You could flavor these in a variety of ways—just use your imagination! Lemon and ginger cream scones might be nice with a cup of tea; just add ½ teaspoon grated ginger (or dry ground) and the zest from 1 lemon. Or fold in ½ cup blueberries or cranberries and add one or two swipes of lemon zest. Or the maple glaze is delicious.

Sour Cream Coffee Cake

This recipe is inspired by my mother. At each family holiday dinner or gathering we'd ask Mom to make her wonderful coffee cake, if she hadn't already thought about it. She knew better. You can also turn this into muffins simply by using muffin tins. It's a versatile recipe for breakfast, afternoon baked goods, or dessert. When my then four-year-old niece Allison visited us at the inn in 2006, she saw my husband take the muffins out of the oven for me and assumed he had made them—hence earning Uncle Greg the nickname, "The Muffin Man"!

Serves 12 to 16

2 sticks plus 2 tablespoons unsalted butter, softened

2 cups granulated sugar

1 cup sour cream

2 eggs

1 tablespoon vanilla extract

2 cups flour

¼ teaspoon salt

1 teaspoon baking powder

1 teaspoon cinnamon

3 tablespoons dark brown sugar

3 tablespoons chopped pecans

1. Preheat the oven to 350 degrees.

2. Combine the 2 sticks of butter and sugar in a mixer and beat with a paddle attachment for about a minute. Add the sour cream and eggs and mix until smooth. Fold in the vanilla, flour, salt, and baking powder. Pour just under half of the batter into a well-greased Bundt pan.

3. Melt the remaining 2 tablespoons of butter and mix it together with the cinnamon, brown sugar, and pecans. Dollop the mixture on top of the batter in the center, taking care not to allow the filling to touch the pan—otherwise it will stick! (Learn from my mistakes.) Layer the remaining batter on top.

4. Bake for 50–60 minutes, until a toothpick comes out clean. Allow to cool completely before removing from the pan. (If you're making muffins, reduce the baking time to 30–35 minutes.)

Dana's Tip
You can also bake this in a large sheet pan and swirl the filling on top; just reduce the cooking time to 30–35 minutes. Make a double batch in a half sheet pan if you need to feed a crowd.

Classic Popovers

I used to make these whenever we'd have family over for brunch before we moved, and I continued the tradition for our inn guests. Jordan Pond House in Acadia National Park serves some great popovers, and their recipe is very close to mine, but our guests said mine hold their own. A technical note: Popover pans are designed specifically with a lip that forces the steam inside the popover to rise up and out to expand, providing its signature balloon-shaped top. Make more than you think you need, as your guests will be happy to enjoy more than one. These are for you, Dad.

Makes 12 to 14

4 large eggs

2 cups whole milk

2 cups flour

1 teaspoon salt

Cinnamon Spice Butter *(see page 190)*

1. Preheat the oven to 400 degrees. Heat popover pan, then coat with nonstick cooking spray.

2. Mix the eggs, milk, flour, and salt in a blender until smooth, scraping down the sides to incorporate all of the flour.

3. Pour the batter into the greased popover pan, filling each indent three-quarters of the way. Bake for 20 minutes. Reduce the heat to 350 degrees and bake for another 10 minutes, or until the top and edges around the rim are brown. Serve with cinnamon spice butter.

Dana's Tip

Do not open the oven at all during cooking to avoid deflating the popovers. If you remove them before the sides have browned enough, they won't hold the weight of the crown and will fall, usually to one side. It's better to overbake a bit than to underbake. Don't get discouraged—it just takes practice to get them right. But the journey to perfection is delicious nonetheless! Try dipping the baked popovers in melted butter and then a mixture of brown sugar and cinnamon. Or if you have a savory preference, place a chunk of Parmesan in the center of the batter and when baked, dip into melted garlic butter!

Raspberry Walnut Rugelach

It's the tender cream cheese dough that makes these so addictive. These have become my husband's new favorite.

Makes about 36 cookies

8 ounces cream cheese, room temperature

2 sticks unsalted butter, room temperature

½ cup granulated sugar, divided

¼ teaspoon kosher salt

1 teaspoon pure vanilla extract

2 cups all-purpose flour

¼ cup light brown sugar, packed

1½ teaspoons ground cinnamon, divided

1 cup walnuts or pecans, finely chopped

½ cup raspberry preserves

1 egg

1 tablespoon milk

Dana's Tip

Note: *These freeze beautifully (before baking)—just freeze flat on a cookie sheet and place in container when frozen. When you're ready to enjoy some, thaw and bake off.*

1. Cream the cream cheese and butter in the bowl of a stand mixer with the paddle attach-ment until light. Add ¼ cup granulated sugar, salt, and vanilla. With the mixer on low speed, add the flour and mix until just combined. Put the dough out onto a well-floured board and roll it into a ball. Cut the ball in quarters, wrap each piece in plastic, and refrigerate for 1 hour.

2. To make the filling, combine about half of the remaining ¼ cup granulated sugar, brown sugar, 1 teaspoon cinnamon, and nuts.

3. On a well-floured board, roll each ball of dough into a 9-inch circle. Spread the dough with 2 tablespoons of the raspberry preserves and sprinkle with ½ cup of the filling. Press the filling lightly into the dough. Cut the circle into quarters, then each quarter into thirds, to create 12 equal wedges. Starting with the wide edge, roll up each wedge. Place the cookies, points tucked under, on a baking sheet lined with parchment paper. Chill for 30 minutes.

4. Preheat the oven to 350 degrees.

5. Beat together the egg and 1 tablespoon milk, then brush each cookie with the egg wash. Combine the remaining granulated sugar and the cinnamon and sprinkle on the cookies. Bake for 15–20 minutes, until lightly browned. Remove to a wire rack and let cool.

Chocolate-Dipped Almond Coconut Macaroons

By now you might have realized that I have an affinity for chocolate! These are double chocolate with cocoa folded into the egg white and coconut mixture. Why? Because a girl can never have too much chocolate.

Makes about 36 macaroons

4 egg whites
¾ cup granulated sugar
1 teaspoon vanilla extract
3 tablespoons cocoa powder
6 tablespoons rice flour
5 cups shredded coconut
1 cup mini chocolate chips
2 cups chocolate melting wafers (or chocolate chips)

1. Preheat the oven to 300 degrees.

2. In a large bowl, beat the egg whites with the sugar and vanilla until frothy, about 2 minutes.

3. Add the cocoa powder and flour and stir until combined. Then beat again for about 30 seconds to 1 minute.

4. Fold in coconut and chocolate chips and mix to coat completely.

5. Using a 2-inch cookie dough scoop, place scoops onto a parchment- or silicone-lined baking sheet and bake until the edges are just lightly browned, 20–25 minutes.

6. While the cookies are cooling, melt the chocolate wafers in a small bowl in the microwave for 1½–2 minutes, stirring after 1 minute and again after another 30 seconds to see if they're fully melted. Dip each macaroon halfway into the melted chocolate and let harden on a sheet of wax paper.

Mini Banana Bundts

This recipe is so easy that I almost didn't include it. But it's a great way to make something basic into a pretty and delicious treat. If you want to make it particularly fancy, drizzle chocolate ganache (*see page 186*) on the cakes once they have cooled.

Makes 8 mini Bundts

¾ cup granulated sugar

¼ cup light brown sugar

½ cup butter, softened
plus 2 tablespoons for
coating the bundt pans

2 tablespoons sour
cream

2 large eggs

3 medium-size ripe
bananas, mashed

1 tablespoon vanilla

1¾ cups cake flour

1 teaspoon baking
powder

½ teaspoon baking soda

¼ teaspoon salt

½ cup mini chocolate
chips (optional)

1. Preheat the oven to 350 degrees.

2. Coat the mini Bundt pans with butter or vegetable oil.

3. Combine the sugars, butter, and sour cream and mix on medium speed until well combined. Add the eggs and continue to mix until smooth. Add the mashed banana and vanilla and mix another few seconds to combine.

4. Fold in the flour, baking powder, baking soda, and salt and mix on low speed until just blended. Be careful not to overmix. Fold in the chocolate chips, if using, and pour into the pans.

5. Bake for 25 minutes in mini Bundt molds. If you don't have mini Bundt molds, you can use a regular pan and bake for 40–45 minutes.

POTATO LATKES,
page 175

CHAPTER 7

Side Dishes

Asparagus and Heirloom Tomato Towers

With microgreens, coarsely cracked black pepper, curry aioli, and cherry tomatoes, this dish makes a nice salad but also a side dish to an egg entrée. The creamy curry aioli is mild and goes really well with the acidity of the tomatoes.

Serves 4

4 ripe heirloom tomatoes (a variety of colors is nice)
8 asparagus spears
Curry Aioli *(see recipe below)*
salt, to taste
coarse cracked black pepper, to taste
microgreens
orange and red cherry tomatoes, halved

1. Slice tomatoes to yield 4 slices per person.
2. Bring a pot of water to a boil and blanch asparagus for about 2 minutes. Remove from water and place in a bowl of ice water to stop the cooking. This keeps the color fresh and texture semicrisp. Let cool.
3. Place a slice of tomato on each plate. Then place 2 halved asparagus spears. Repeat layer with each remaining plate. Top with curry aioli, salt, pepper, and microgreens. Garnish plate with halved cherry tomatoes.

Curry Aioli

1 cup mayonnaise
1 tablespoon honey
1 teaspoon yellow curry powder
juice of ½ a lime
½ teaspoon salt

To make the curry aioli:

Combine the mayonnaise, honey, curry powder, lime juice, and salt in a food processor until smooth. (You could mix this by hand—just be sure to mix thoroughly.) Refrigerate for 8 hours or as long as overnight to allow the flavors to meld before serving. Store in a squeeze bottle in the refrigerator up to 3 weeks.

Roasted Fennel Bulbs

This vegetable, with its licorice flavor profile, is not for everyone. But caramelize it with garlic-infused olive oil and some of your guests might just change their minds. It makes a great accompaniment to eggs, particularly topped with freshly shaved Parmesan cheese.

Serves 4

2 fennel bulbs

¼ cup extra-virgin olive oil

3 cloves garlic, smashed

1 teaspoon coarse kosher salt

½ teaspoon freshly ground black pepper

4-ounce block of Parmesan cheese

1 lemon, for garnish

1. Preheat the oven to 375 degrees.

2. Halve each fennel bulb vertically, keeping the core intact to hold the bulb together while roasting.

3. In a small saucepan, add the olive oil and smashed garlic and cook over medium-low heat for 5 minutes. Remove garlic and drizzle the olive oil all over the bulbs. Sprinkle with salt and pepper. Roast the fennel cut side down on a baking sheet until caramelized and brown, about 45 minutes, covering with foil after 30 minutes.

4. To serve, cut and remove the core (following the V shape of the core). Using a vegetable peeler, shave a few shards of Parmesan on top of each bulb and serve with a lemon wedge.

Sweet Potato Latkes

Makes about 12 four-inch latkes (gluten free)

2 large sweet potatoes, peeled

1 medium sweet onion

2 large eggs

¾ cup rice flour

1½ teaspoons baking powder

1 teaspoon salt

¼ teaspoon freshly ground black pepper

¼ teaspoon yellow curry powder

2 cups vegetable oil, for frying (or enough to come up about ¼ inch
  from the bottom of the pan)

1. In a food processor using the medium shredding disc, process the potatoes and onion, then place in a towel and squeeze to remove moisture. Place in large mixing bowl. Add the eggs, flour, baking powder, salt, pepper, and curry powder and mix until well blended.

2. In large frying pan, heat vegetable oil until hot. Take about ⅓ cup of the mixture and shape it into a flat disc as best you can, then carefully add to the oil, trying to keep the round shape. Fry until brown on one side, about 3–4 minutes. Flip, cooking another 3 minutes until browned. Remove to a paper towel. Repeat until all the pancakes are fried. You can keep them warm in a 250-degree oven until ready to serve.

Classic Potato Latkes

Makes about 12 4-inch latkes (gluten free)

2 large russet or Idaho potatoes, skin on

1 medium sweet onion

2 large eggs

½ cup rice flour

1½ teaspoons baking powder

1 teaspoon salt

¼ teaspoon freshly ground black pepper

½ teaspoon onion powder

2 cups vegetable oil for frying (or enough to come up about ¼ inch
    from the bottom of the pan)

1. In a food processor using the medium (or large versus small if you don't have a
   medium) shredding disc, process the potatoes and onion, then place in a towel and
   squeeze to remove moisture. Place in large mixing bowl. Add the eggs, flour, baking
   powder, salt, pepper, and onion powder and mix until well blended.

2. In a large frying pan, heat vegetable oil until hot. Take about ⅓ cup of the mixture and
   shape it into a flat disc as best you can, then carefully add to the oil, trying to keep its
   round shape. Fry until brown on one side, about 3–4 minutes. Flip, cooking another
   3 minutes until browned. Remove to a paper towel. Repeat until all the pancakes are
   fried. You can keep them warm in a 250-degree oven until ready to serve, or keep
   them at room temperature for an hour or so and quick-reheat at 375 before serving.

Roasted Potato Wedges *with* Horseradish Sour Cream

The key to getting a crispy potato outside with a creamy center is soaking them in salt water the night before and baking them on high heat in olive oil. This removes much of the starch, yielding a crispy baked "fry."

Serves 4

1 tablespoon plus 1 teaspoon salt

4 cups warm water

2 large baking potatoes, scrubbed, skin on

¼ cup extra-virgin olive oil

1 teaspoon granulated garlic

2 tablespoons grated Parmesan cheese

1 pint sour cream

1 tablespoon bottled horseradish

1 tablespoon Dijon mustard

2 tablespoons chopped fresh chives

1. Dissolve 1 tablespoon salt in 4 cups of warm water in a large bowl.

2. Cut the potatoes lengthwise into 8 wedges and add to the salt water. Refrigerate in water overnight, or for at least 8 hours prior to baking.

3. When ready to bake, preheat the oven to 400 degrees.

4. Drain the potatoes thoroughly. Add ½ teaspoon salt, olive oil, garlic, and grated Parmesan to the potatoes and toss to coat. Spread on a rimmed baking sheet and bake until browned, about 45–50 minutes.

5. While the potatoes are baking, mix the sour cream, horseradish, mustard, the remaining ½ teaspoon salt, and chives and set aside until ready to serve. (Making this the day before allows the flavor to really develop.) Divide the wedges among 4 plates and serve with a couple of tablespoons of the horseradish sour cream in a small ramekin or condiment cup. I would serve these along side several of my egg dishes, but it's really, once they are done, enjoy however or with whatever!

Black Pepper Candied Bacon

Make extra. Period.

Serves 6

12 strips thick-cut bacon

4 tablespoons brown sugar

black pepper, for sprinkling

1. Preheat the oven to 350 degrees.

2. Place bacon directly on a baking sheet. Coat evenly with the brown sugar, rubbing it in a bit. Sprinkle very generously with black pepper. Cook until bacon turns a very dark brown-burgundy color and the sugar has become shiny like a hard candy. It will almost look burnt, but will appear more dark burgundy than black. If it's black, it's too late. (Remove it from the oven just prior to that! I tend to check mine every couple minutes once it starts to get dark.) Place on dry sheet pan—do not put on a towel, the sugar will cause it to stick!—and let cool a few minutes to allow the sugar to harden.

Beets and Goat Cheese with Orange Vinaigrette

I like to make this featuring a local goat cheese and orange vinaigrette using Fiore's blood orange extra-virgin olive oil. Use your favorite local goat cheese and follow the instructions below if you don't have the Fiore oil.

Serves 4 to 6

3 large red beets

6 ounces goat cheese

¼ cup olive oil

½ teaspoon pure orange extract

1 tablespoon balsamic vinegar

salt, to taste

freshly ground black pepper, to taste

2 thyme sprigs

1. Preheat the oven to 375 degrees.

2. Peel the beets and wrap in nonstick foil. Roast in the oven for 45 minutes to 1 hour, until tender. Let cool, then slice into ⅛–¼-inch rounds.

3. Mix the olive oil, orange extract, and vinegar with a dash of salt and pepper and the leaves from 1 sprig of thyme.

4. To serve, layer the sliced beets with a tablespoon of goat cheese spread between. Drizzle with the vinaigrette, and garnish with a few fresh thyme leaves.

BLACK PEPPER
CANDIED BACON,
page 177

**BEETS AND
GOAT CHEESE,**
page 177

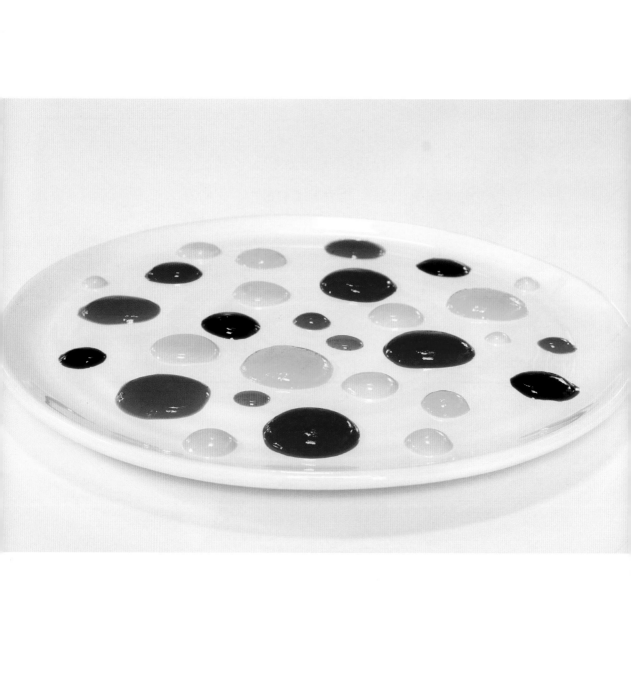

CHAPTER 8

Condiments
and Sauces

Simple Syrup

Makes approximately 2¼ cups

2 cups sugar
1½ cups cold water
2 tablespoons white corn syrup

Combine the sugar, water, and corn syrup in a medium saucepan and cook over medium-high heat for about 10 minutes, until all the sugar is completely dissolved. Do not allow the syrup to boil. Remove from heat and allow the syrup to cool completely before using. When cool, pour into a container and store in the refrigerator up to 3 weeks or the freezer for up to 3 months.

Note: The purpose of the corn syrup is to keep the sugar from crystallizing, which can cause a grainy syrup.

Basil Simple Syrup

Makes approximately 2¼ cups

2 cups sugar
1½ cups cold water
2 tablespoons corn syrup
¼ cup packed fresh basil leaves

1. Combine the sugar, water, and corn syrup in a medium saucepan and cook over medium-high heat for about 10 minutes, until all the sugar is completely dissolved. Do not allow the syrup to come to a boil.

2. While the sugar is cooking, finely chop the basil and place half in a mesh bag or loose-tea steeper and place into the sugar mixture. Set the other half aside.

3. When slightly cooled, remove cooked basil, add fresh basil, and chill. This will keep refrigerated up to 2 months or 6 months in the freezer.

Hibiscus Simple Syrup

A wonderful Maine resource for hibiscus petals is SKORDO, at skordo.com.

Makes approximately 2¼ cups

2 cups sugar

1½ cups cold water

2 tablespoons white corn syrup

¼ cup dried hibiscus flowers

Combine all ingredients in medium saucepan and cook over medium heat for about 5 minutes, until all the sugar is completely dissolved. Once the sugar just comes to a boil, lower to simmer and continue to cook on low for 5 minutes. Turn off the heat and let sit and steep for at least 30 minutes. When cool, strain and pour into a storage container or squeeze bottle and refrigerate until ready to use. This will keep refrigerated up to 2 months or 6 months in the freezer.

Cranberry, Honey, and Rosemary Simple Syrup

Makes approximately 2½ cups

½ cup whole cranberries

1 cup sugar

1 cup honey

1 cup cold water

2 sprigs rosemary

In a small saucepan, add the cranberries and smash with a muddler or the bottom of a heavy glass. Add the sugar, honey, water, and rosemary and cook over medium heat for about 5 minutes, until all the sugar is completely dissolved and honey is fully incorporated. When cool, strain through a fine-mesh sieve and pour into a storage container or squeeze bottle and refrigerate until ready to use. This will keep refrigerated for up to 1 month or 3 months in the freezer.

Earl Grey Simple Syrup

This is delicious over fruit or yogurt and on pound cake.

Makes approximately 2¼ cups

2 cups sugar

1½ cups cold water

2 tablespoons white corn syrup

4 Earl Grey tea bags

Combine the sugar, water, and corn syrup in medium saucepan and cook over medium heat for about 5 minutes, until all the sugar is completely dissolved. Once the sugar just comes to a boil, lower to simmer and add the tea bags. Continue to cook on low for 5 minutes. Turn off heat and let sit and steep for at least 30 minutes. When cool, pour into a storage container or squeeze bottle and refrigerate until ready to use.

Green Tea Mint–Infused Simple Syrup

Makes approximately 2¼ cups

2 cups sugar

1⅓ cups cold water

1 tablespoon white corn syrup

¼ cup packed fresh mint leaves

1 green tea bag

1. Combine the sugar, water, and corn syrup in a medium saucepan and cook over medium-high heat for about 10 minutes, until all the sugar is completely dissolved. Do not allow the syrup to come to a full rolling boil.

2. While the sugar is cooking, finely chop the mint and place half in mesh bag or loose-tea steeper and place into sugar mixture. Set the other half aside.

3. Remove from heat, add the tea bag, and allow the syrup to cool completely. When cool, remove the mint and tea bag and add the remainder of the fresh mint. This will keep refrigerated up to 2 months or 6 months in the freezer.

Maple Rum Sauce

Makes 2 cups

1½ cups heavy cream
⅓ cup packed dark brown sugar
¼ cup maple syrup
⅓ cup plus 3 tablespoons spiced rum
3 teaspoons cornstarch

1. Combine the cream, brown sugar, maple syrup, and ⅓ cup rum in a medium saucepan and bring to a slow boil over low heat. Dissolve the cornstarch in the remaining 3 tablespoons of rum. Whisk the cornstarch mixture into the saucepan, lower the heat, and cook for another 2 minutes, until thickened. Remove from the heat and let cool.

2. When cool, store in the refrigerator for 4–5 days or freeze for up to 3 weeks. (If freezing, leave room at the top of the squeeze bottle or any storage container for expansion.) Simply reheat in the microwave on low if you want to serve it warm over ice cream or in hot coffee!

Rhubarb Sauce

Makes about 2½ cups

4 cups chopped fresh rhubarb
½ cup water
½ cup granulated sugar

Add the rhubarb, water, and sugar in a medium saucepan and cook, covered, for 15–20 minutes, until soft. Remove from the heat and puree with an immersion or standard blender until smooth. Serve immediately or let cool and refrigerate until ready to use. If refrigerating, warm in the microwave before serving. This can be stored in the refrigerator for up to 3 days or in the freezer for 4 weeks. (If freezing, leave room at the top of the squeeze bottle or any storage container for expansion.)

Chocolate Ganache

Makes about 2 cups

1½ cups heavy cream

1 cup dark brown sugar

8 ounces bittersweet (up to 70% cocoa) chocolate (shaved or chips)

½ stick unsalted butter

3 tablespoons dark rum

1 teaspoon vanilla extract

Combine all ingredients in a small saucepan and heat over medium-low heat until the chocolate is completely melted and combined. Use a whisk and stir constantly for best results. Cool completely and store in refrigerator for up to 1 week or in freezer for 1 month. (If freezing, leave room at the top of the squeeze bottle or any storage container for expansion.) To reheat, thaw in refrigerator and then let the bottle sit upright in a hot water bath or pour into a double boiler to warm slowly over a low simmer.

Raspberry Coulis

Makes about 2 cups

1 24-ounce bag frozen raspberries, thawed and with
   most of the visible excess liquid drained

1 tablespoon fresh lemon juice

½ cup powdered sugar

Combine all ingredients in a blender and puree for about 20 seconds. Push through a fine-mesh sieve or a strainer. Store in a plastic airtight container in the refrigerator for up to 1 week or in the freezer for up to 4 weeks. (If freezing, leave room at the top of the squeeze bottle or any storage container for expansion.)

Blackberry Coulis

Makes about 2 cups

1 24-ounce bag frozen blackberries, thawed and with
  most of the visible excess liquid drained
1 tablespoon fresh lemon juice
½ cup powdered sugar

Combine all ingredients in a blender and puree for about 20 seconds. Push through
a fine-mesh sieve or a strainer. Store in a plastic airtight container in the refrigerator
for up to 1 week or in the freezer for up to 4 weeks. (If freezing, leave room at the
top of the squeeze bottle or any storage container for expansion.)

Mango Coulis

Makes about 2¼ cups

1 24-ounce bag frozen mango, thawed and with
  most of the visible excess liquid drained
1 tablespoon fresh lemon juice
½ cup powdered sugar

Combine all ingredients in a blender and puree for about 20 seconds. Push through
a fine-mesh sieve or a strainer. Store in a plastic airtight container in the refrigerator
for up to 1 week or in the freezer for up to 4 weeks. (If freezing, leave room at the
top of the squeeze bottle or any storage container for expansion.)

Coconut Lime Crème

This sauce is wonderful on a variety of tropical fruits. I particularly love it with watermelon and kiwi. This sauce also freezes well. (If freezing, leave room at the top of the squeeze bottle or any storage container for expansion.)

Makes about 2 cups

1 pint sour cream

½ cup canned coconut milk

½ teaspoon coconut extract

½ cup powdered sugar

zest of 1 lime

Combine all ingredients in a blender and puree for about 10 seconds. Scrape down the sides and blend again for another few seconds. Store in a container in the refrigerator for up to 1 week or in the freezer for up to 4 weeks. (If freezing, leave room at the top of the squeeze bottle or any storage container for expansion.)

Cinnamon Crème

Not only is this one of the easiest sauces you can make to accompany fresh fruit, but it's also one that can stand up to the heat of a torch to create the classic brûlée topping. The key is the sour cream—it won't curdle or cook when torched the way a brûlée custard with eggs would. It freezes well, too. (If freezing, leave room at the top of the squeeze bottle or any storage container for expansion. When thawed, it will appear to have separated, but vigorously shake and it will blend right back together.)

Makes about 2 cups

1 pint sour cream

1 tablespoon ground cinnamon

2 tablespoons honey

4 tablespoons heavy cream

¹/₃ cup dark brown sugar

Combine all ingredients in a blender and puree for about 10 seconds. Scrape down the sides and blend again for another few seconds. Store in a container in the refrigerator for up to 1 week or in the freezer for up to 4 weeks. (If freezing, leave room at the top of the squeeze bottle or any storage container for expansion. When thawed, it will appear to have separated, but vigorously shake and it will blend right back together.)

Vanilla Bean Crème

This sauce can actually be used to accompanying many fruits, scones, angel food cake, pound cake, or ice cream!

Makes about 2 cups

1 pint sour cream
1 tablespoon vanilla extract
seeds from 1 vanilla bean
2 tablespoons honey
4 tablespoons heavy cream
⅓ cup granulated sugar

1. Combine the sour cream, vanilla extract, vanilla bean seeds, honey, heavy cream, and sugar in a blender and puree for about 10 seconds. Scrape down the sides and blend again for another few seconds. Store in a container in the refrigerator for up to 1 week or in the freezer for about 4 weeks. (If freezing, leave room at the top of the squeeze bottle or any storage container for expansion. When thawed, it will appear to have separated, but vigorously shake and it will blend right back together.)

Chive and Scallion Butter

This is simply delicious on eggs and savory popovers.

Makes a little over ½ cup

1 stick butter, softened
1 tablespoon fresh chopped chives
2 scallion stalks, trimmed one inch from each end, very thinly sliced
½ teaspoon salt

In a small bowl, using a rubber spatula, combine all ingredients until well blended. Roll into a log shape and wrap in plastic. Refrigerate until ready to use. Use as you would regular butter. Keeps in the refrigerator for up to 1 week or in the freezer for 5 months.

Cinnamon Spice Butter

Makes a little over ½ cup

1 stick unsalted butter, softened
2 tablespoons powdered sugar
1 tablespoon ground cinnamon
¼ teaspoon ground cloves

In a small bowl, using a rubber spatula, combine the butter and sugar, then add the cinnamon and cloves and mix until smooth. Refrigerate until ready to use. Use as you would regular butter. Keeps in the refrigerator for up to 2 weeks or in the freezer for 5 months.

Chive Oil

Makes a little over ½ cup

1 large bunch (about an inch or more in diameter) fresh chives, sliced in half
¼ cup light olive oil
¼ cup grapeseed or vegetable oil
¼ teaspoon salt

1. Bring a saucepan of water to a boil. Add the chives and blanch for 10–15 seconds. Drain and transfer to an ice bath. Remove and pat dry on paper towels, squeezing to remove any excess water. Roughly chop a bit more and transfer to a blender. With the blender running, add the oils and salt through the opening and process until smooth.

2. Transfer to a bowl and refrigerate overnight. Let come to room temperature and strain through a fine-mesh strainer. Transfer to a squeeze bottle and refrigerate until needed, for up to 1 week. (Bring to room temperature before using.)

Smoked Paprika Oil

Makes ½ cup

½ cup extra-virgin olive oil
2 teaspoons smoked paprika
fleur de sel sea salt

Heat the olive oil over medium heat in a small skillet or saucepan until tiny bubbles appear around the edge. Remove from heat and stir in smoked paprika and a good pinch of sea salt. Whisk really well to combine. Let come to room temperature and strain through a fine-mesh strainer. Transfer to a squeeze bottle and refrigerate until needed, for up to 1 week. (Bring to room temperature before using.)

Cranberry Bourbon
Spritzer,
page 199

CHAPTER 9

Simple Cocktails

for Brunch and

Beyond

Cucumber and Basil Lemon Spritzer

2 slices cucumber

2 ounces vodka

¾ ounce limoncello

¾ ounce fresh lemon juice

¾ ounce Basil Simple Syrup *(see page 182)*

club soda

basil sprig, for garnish

cucumber wheel, for garnish

Add cucumber to a cocktail shaker and muddle. Add vodka, limoncello, lemon juice, and simple syrup, and fill halfway with ice and shake. Strain and pour into a tall rocks glass filled with ice. Top with club soda. Garnish with fresh basil sprig and a cucumber wheel.

Elderflower Cosmo

1½ ounces vodka

½ ounce St. Germain liquor

¾ ounce cranberry juice

¾ ounce fresh lime juice

lime wheel, for garnish

Mix all ingredients and shake over ice. Pour into martini or coupe glass and garnish with a lime wheel float.

Strawberry Gin Mojito

4 ripe strawberries, stems removed, plus one with stem for garnish

4 fresh mint leaves

2 ounces gin

¾ ounce fresh lemon juice

1 ounce Simple Syrup *(see page 182)*

club soda

mint sprig, for garnish

Muddle strawberries with mint in a cocktail shaker. Fill halfway with ice, then add gin, lemon juice, and simple syrup and shake. Strain into a tall rocks glass filled with ice and top with club soda, a strawberry and a mint sprig.

The Earl Grey

2 ounces gin

¾ ounce fresh lemon juice

¾ ounce Earl Grey Simple Syrup *(see page 184)*

3 dashes lemongrass bitters

lemon wheel, for garnish garnish

rosemary sprig, for garnish garnish

Mix all ingredients and fill shaker halfway with ice and shake. Pour into martini or coupe glass and garnish with a lemon wheel and a sprig of rosemary.

The Sweet Tart

This does taste like a SweeTart!

5 blackberries

2 ounces gin

1 ounce Chambord

¾ ounce fresh lemon juice

blackberry, for garnish

lemon wheel, for garnish

Muddle blackberries in a cocktail shaker. Add gin, Chambord, and lemon juice, fill halfway with ice and shake. Pour into martini or coupe glass and garnish with a blackberry and lemon wheel.

Cranberry Bourbon Spritzer

Not too sweet, not too tart—this makes a beautiful and festive brunch or holiday cocktail!

8 cranberries, plus a few for garnish

1½ ounces bourbon

1 ounce Cranberry, Honey, and Rosemary Simple Syrup *(see page 183)*

club soda

rosemary sprig, for garnish

Muddle the cranberries in a cocktail shaker. Add the bourbon, simple syrup, and fill halfway with ice. Shake until cold. Pour into a short rocks glass over ice, top with club soda, and garnish with a few fresh cranberries and a rosemary sprig.

Hibiscus Gin Fizz

4 ounces dry Prosecco

1 ounce gin

1 ounce Hibiscus Simple Syrup *(see page 183)*

½ ounce fresh lime juice

4 dashes of hibiscus water

raspberries, for garnish

mint sprig, for garnish

Mix Prosecco, gin, simple syrup, lime, and hibiscus water in cocktail shaker over ice. Pour into a champagne flute. Garnish with a mint sprig and a few raspberries.

Pineapple Rum Sour

2x2-inch wedge of fresh pineapple

2 ounces amber rum (I like Mount Gay)

¾ ounce St. Germain liquor

½ ounce fresh lemon juice

½ ounce fresh lime juice

mint sprig, for garnish

pineapple wedge, for garnish

Muddle the pineapple in a cocktail shaker. Add remaining ingredients and shake over ice. Strain and serve in a short rocks glass over ice. Garnish with a sprig of mint and a pineapple wedge.

Smokin' Bloody Maria

¾ teaspoon smoked paprika, divided

½ teaspoon smoked sea salt

¼ teaspoon black pepper

1 cup Homemade Bloody Mary Mix, chilled *(see recipe below)*

2 ounces mezcal

1 ounce Roasted Brown Sugar Jalapeño–Infused Tequila *(see recipe below)*

1 ounce Herradura Silver tequila

½ ounce fresh lime juice

2 lime wedges, for garnish

2 cherry tomatoes, for garnish

4 spicy dilly beans, for garnish

2 fresh jalapeño slices, for garnish

Mix together ½ teaspoon each of smoked paprika and smoked sea salt and ½ teaspoon of black pepper. Run a cut lime around the rim of two glasses and dip the rim into the spice mixture. Add ice to the glasses. Mix all other ingredients (including the remaining ¼ teaspoon of smoked paprika) and pour into the glasses. Garnish each glass with a lime wedge, cherry tomato, spicy dilly beans, and a fresh jalapeño slice.

Homemade Bloody Mary Mix

2 cups tomato juice

1½ teaspoons lemon juice

2 tablespoons Worcestershire sauce

1½ tablespoons sriracha

1 teaspoon kosher salt

Mix all ingredients until well blended.

Roasted Brown Sugar Jalapeño–Infused Tequila

2 fresh jalapeños

2 tablespoons light brown sugar

1 cup Herradura Silver tequila

To make the roasted brown sugar jalapeño–infused tequila:

On a sheet pan, broil the jalapeños until they are nicely charred and blistered. Then turn the oven to 425 degrees, add the brown sugar to the jalapeños, and roast for 15–18 minutes. Let them cool and add them (and the caramelized brown sugar in the pan) to the tequila in a jar. Let sit for at least a couple of days before using, to allow the flavors to meld. The longer you infuse the tequila, the spicier it will be.

Layered Chocolate Cherry Cocktail

This is truly a dessert cocktail.

2 tablespoons Chocolate Ganache, room temperature *(see page 186)*
2 tablespoons Maple Rum Sauce, chilled *(see page 185)*
2 ounces chocolate liqueur
¾ ounces vanilla vodka
¾ ounces Luxardo cherry liqueur
dark cherries, for garnish

Add the chocolate ganache to a martini glass, then slowly add the rum sauce on top of the chocolate layer. Shake the chocolate liqueur, vanilla vodka, and cherry liqueur over ice and strain. Pour into the martini glass slowly over the back of a spoon so the other two layers don't separate. Garnish with dark cherries.

Hot Spiced Coffee

4 ounces dark brewed hot coffee

1½ ounce bourbon

2 ounce spiced rum

3 dashes of molasses bitters

about ¼ cup Fresh Whipped Cream
   (see recipe below)

Chocolate Ganache, for drizzling
   (see page 186)

Mix the hot coffee, bourbon, rum, and molasses bitters and pour into clear coffee glass. Top with whipped cream and drizzle with chocolate ganache.

Fresh Whipped Cream

1 pint heavy whipping cream

3 tablespoons powdered sugar

1 teaspoon vanilla extract

To make whipped cream:

Beat cream, sugar, and vanilla in a stand mixer until stiff, being careful not to overmix or the cream will separate.

Dark Espresso Martini

Maple Rum Sauce, chilled *(see page 185)*

1 ounce brewed espresso (espresso roast brewed drip coffee will also work; just make it dark)

1 ounce espresso-infused vodka

1 fresh vanilla bean, seeds scraped and set aside

½ ounce Amaro Montenegro

½ ounce coffee brandy

½ ounce Kahlua

espresso beans, for garnish

Using a squeeze bottle, drizzle the chilled rum sauce on the inside of a martini glass. Mix espresso, vodka, vanilla bean seeds, Amaro Montenegro, brandy, and Kahlua over ice in a cocktail shaker and strain into the martini glass. Garnish with espresso beans. You could also dip the rim in the rum sauce and then into crushed espresso beans.

Hot Tea Toddy

This is my twist on a recipe from Split Rock Distillery.

1 good-quality black tea bag
2 ounces bourbon
1 ounce maple syrup
4 dashes of black walnut bitters
orange peel, for garnish

Add the tea bag and boiling water to a clear mug. Add bourbon, maple syrup, and bitters and let steep for 3–4 minutes. Garnish with orange peel.

CHAPTER 9

Garnishing
and Plating

Garnishing and Plating

I think we can all agree that we first eat with our eyes. So why not decorate your plate and frame your subject as you would a window, a piece of wall art, or a table? Garnishing a plate can be one of the nicest ways to indicate that you care about what you are giving your guests. You've thought about ways to enhance the appeal of your dish in ways that are far beyond an orange wedge, and a piece of curly parsley as a garnish. And please, no dried parsley sprinkles! Here are some simple ways to dress up your dish.

On the base of the plate:

- Baby spinach, baby arugula, or mixed greens
  When I think about plating any dish, I first consider the base. With a savory dish, I prefer to use a white plate and start with fresh greens, particularly when serving something without much contrasting color.

Around the plate:

- Finely diced or julienned red, orange, and yellow bell peppers
  Scatter the diced version around the plate or pile up the julienned on top of a dish. If you aren't plating with any greens, add a green bell pepper for more contrast.

- Thinly shaved radishes and carrots
  Just a pop of crunch and fresh color.

- Aioli dots, drizzles, or swooshes
  Fun for a pop of color and as a dip for fresh veggies or your bell pepper garnish.

- Cherry tomato halves
  Scatter both orange and red for a fresh pop of color that also go really well with the aioli, chive oil, smoked paprika oil, or balsamic.

- Chocolate sauce
  Use in dots, random drizzles, or even to spell words on the plate (Happy Birthday, Bon Appetit, etc.).

- Fruit coulis
  In dots or random patterns.

- Smoked paprika oil, chive oil, vinaigrette, or balsamic glaze
  A couple swirls around the plate can add interest and flavor.

On top of your plated dish:

- Fresh dill fronds or fennel fronds
  These add a lacy, airy pop of color as well as height to a dish.

- Crispy fried shallots
  These add a nice crunch element to a variety of egg dishes.

- Microgreens
  These can give a pop of color, adding height and fresh crunch to the dish.

- Finely minced chives
  Chives are a delicious pop of color to most any egg dish!

- Fresh mint sprigs (sweet dish), rosemary or thyme sprig or basil leaves
  (savory entrée)
  Don't use just the leaf, but the top section of 2 or 3 sections of leaves or a whole sprig.

- Edible flowers
  These are simply beautiful. Nasturtiums grow well in pots and come in various colors. If you're going to garnish with a flower, it really should be edible.

How about a side dish bite as a garnish?

- Smoked Salmon, Cream Cheese, and Cucumber Roulade (*see page 22*)

- Smoked Salmon Caviar, Horseradish Crème Fraiche, and Fresh Dill on
  Cucumber or Zucchini Rounds (*see page 21*) under savory small bites

- Tomato, Ricotta, and Swiss Tarts (*see page 31*)

- Mini version of the Salad Lyonnaise (*see page 24*)

- A small Beets and Goat Cheese with Orange Vinaigrette (*see page 177*)

Hot Tea Toddy,
page 207

RECIPE INDEX

ABOUT THE AUTHOR

Dana Moos is a former innkeeper who found great pleasure in creating unique and delicious meals for her guests. She is now a broker specializing in inns and B&Bs, and lives in midcoast Maine.